The President: Rex,
Princeps, Imperator?

The President:
Rex, Princeps, Imperator?

Selected Papers from Symposia
on the 1968 Presidential Election

Edited by

JOSEPH M. RAY
H. Y. Benedict Professor of Political Science
The University of Texas at El Paso

〜〜〜〜〜〜〜〜〜〜〜〜〜〜〜〜〜〜〜〜〜

TEXAS WESTERN PRESS

THE UNIVERSITY OF TEXAS AT EL PASO

1969

RICHARD M. NIXON
Republican
Vice-President of the United States, 1952-1960

SPIRO T. AGNEW
Republican
Governor of Maryland

HUBERT H. HUMPHREY
Democrat
Vice-President of the United States

EDMUND S. MUSKIE
Democrat
United States Senator from Maine

LYNDON B. JOHNSON
Democrat
President of the United States

GEORGE C. WALLACE
American Party
Former Governor of Alabama

CURTIS LEMAY
American Party
Retired Air Force General

ROBERT F. KENNEDY
Democrat
United States Senator from New York

EUGENE MCCARTHY
Democrat
United States Senator from Minnesota

GEORGE MCGOVERN
Democrat
United States Senator from South Dakota

RONALD REAGAN
Republican
Governor of California

GEORGE W. ROMNEY
Republican
Governor of Michigan

NELSON A. ROCKEFELLER
Republican
Governor of New York

CONTENTS

PREFACE

THE VIEWS of scholars expressed concerning the 1968 Presidential Campaign while the Campaign was in progress are in large measure overcome by events. These views are of interest now, not because they predicted events to come, but because they demonstrated in scholarly detail the difficulties of discussing candidates, issues, unforeseen events, and the vagaries of the American voter. The weekly reports of the poll-taking organizations have now greatly influenced the ordinary voter's decision-making process. He is not sure whether to get on the bandwagon or to seek his independent judgment. Consequently, the number of undecided voters in 1968 remained in large percentage up until election day. The closeness of the final popular vote is proof that many Americans were torn in their loyalties until they entered the polling booth.

No effort has been made by the various authors to change their pronouncements as originally made at the symposia. This fact makes a reading now attractive, because it discloses the complexities that arose after President Johnson announced on March 31, 1968, his decision not to run. Here and there we see side glimpses of the attitudes of scholars in forecasting problems prior to the event. Some of these relate to racial relations, urban renewal, and the enormous difficulties of bringing the war in Vietnam to an honorable conclusion.

As we study the way President Nixon now conducts the office of the Presidency, we have for the most part forgotten the torments that beset us when candidates like Senator McCarthy, Governor George Wallace, and Senator George McGovern announced themselves as spokesmen for minority views. It is a commentary on the ability of the American people to reunite even after a very close election. There is thus, in our view, substantial value in recording the opinions and projections of competent scholars dated in time months or only weeks before the election itself.

The funds for the three symposia were provided by The University of Texas at El Paso under the leadership of President Joseph M. Ray, and after his retirement by Acting President Milton Leech. From the beginning we understood and accepted the relationship between the art of politics and the art of rhetoric. Aristotle was among the first to remind us of this affinity. Incidentally, modern specialization has led us to neglect the view that a man speaking in his own behalf is still the central figure in an election campaign. Without him the news media, the managers, and all those who like to consider themselves experts would have practically nothing upon which to make their judgments. These papers reflect the ways in which various political leaders seeking election have affected political scientists and rhetorical scholars in projecting their personalities upon the American voter.

It is hoped that symposia of this kind will become a quadrennial feature of the program of The University of Texas at El Paso. Surely no one can disagree with the idea that democracy survives only with the aid of large numbers of well-informed voters and candidates with high principles. The study of issues and candidates is no longer a responsibility that can be discharged in a few days once every four years. It requires continuous, day to day, serious study and reflection.

— HAROLD F. HARDING

El Paso: June, 1969

ABOUT THE SYMPOSIA

THE ADDRESSES published here are those for which publishable manuscripts were presented by participants in two symposia on the 1968 Presidential Campaign at The University of Texas at El Paso in April, 1968, and September, 1968. A total of fifteen scholars spent six days in analyzing the campaign. Among the other distinguished persons who participated were Democratic Senator Lee Metcalf of Montana; Malcolm C. Moos, formerly with the Ford Foundation and now President of the University of Minnesota; Samuel Lubell, public opinion analyst and columnist, member of the faculty in journalism at Columbia University, and author of *The Future of American Politics;* Bruce L. Felknor, Assistant to William Benton of the *Encyclopaedia Britannica* and author of *Dirty Politics;* Warren E. Miller of the Survey Research Center at the University of Michigan; and William Roberts of Spencer-Roberts in Los Angeles.

This volume, like the three symposia, could not have been produced without the generous advice and assistance of the Departments of Political Science and Speech. We wish to thank in particular Dr. Theodore O. Windt, Jr., then Associate Professor of Speech; Dr. Gifford W. Wingate, Head of the Department of Speech; Dr. Kenneth E. Beasley, then Head of the Department of Political Science and now Graduate Dean; Dr. Thomas Ira Cook, H. Y. Benedict Profesor of Political Science; and Dr. Clyde Wingfield, Head of the U. T. E. P. Department of Political Science in 1967 and now McElvaney Professor at Southern Methodist University. They made substantial contributions to the organization and conduct of the symposia.

—JOSEPH M. RAY

El Paso: June, 1969

I

THE PRESIDENT: REX, PRINCEPS, IMPERATOR?

by

JASPER B. SHANNON

University of Nebraska

September, 1968

THE AMERICAN PRESIDENCY, *personified in Washington for whom it was in large part originally designed, derived from the concept of monarchy: thus Rex; as parties developed and matured, party leadership fell naturally into whatever presidential hands were capable of seizing and exercising it: hence Princeps; and, with the role of commander in chief and chief of state, as the nation's involvement in world affairs burgeoned, came: Imperator.*

Nearly all of Professor Shannon's paper is devoted to roles played by the succession of presidents in accordance with these criteria. The author's flowing eloquence rides a rising crest, until, with the end of his catalog of the Odyssean ships, he offers us a supreme intellectual challenge: "Can the office of president survive? Is it, like the doctrine of separation of powers, doomed, impaled upon the theology of the trinity? Can anyone less versatile than a combination of Jesus Christ and Julius Caesar with parts of Napoleon added successfully fill an office with standards requiring the talents of a rex, *a* princeps *and an* imperator *united in one and perform tasks requiring not only charismatic but even divine powers?"*

• POLITICAL INSTITUTIONS are the creations of the minds and emotions of men in response to their felt needs — real or imaginary. Born an inadequate animal in a not always friendly environment, the human organism builds up patterns of behavior as the nervous system responds to the stimuli of physical nature. From birth to death puny man seeks security and postponement of his inevitable annihilation. Either from nature or from nature's God he inherits a yearning for immortality, both spiritual and biological. The weakest of all among the animal young, his prolonged dependency upon his elders, as Plato emphasized centuries ago, makes him a social being. To protect themselves from other animals and from the most predatory of all, their fellow human beings, men associate in groups compelled to communicate by sounds and symbols that eventually link the living with the dead and the remote past with the unseen future. Aggressive beings because of their fears must exercise collective power both to preserve themselves by mutual aid and to attack others to enlarge their resources in a world of scarce resources and ruthless competition for existence.

These necessities inherent in man's imperfect nature are reflected in his social institutions. To survive at all there must be an *ordo;* some kind of natural or created form of organization is essential to living at all as Aristotle put it or to living well after the assurance of survival. Man's freedom depends upon the absence of the chaos described by Thomas Hobbes where life is "short, nasty and brutish." The strongest man has not only the power to withstand his enemies but to maintain order for others. Either Hercules or Odysseus, one by brute strength, and the other by physical skill linked to cunning use of words including the art of propaganda. The "honey tongued" Greek hero is the father of the legal profession and the model of a public relations counsel. Craft often outwits pure physical power, *vide* Samson and all his male descendants who allow themselves to be seduced by feminine wiles.

Incurably worshipful, the human animal seeks objects of worship either in creatures of nature (some monstrous in shape and form) or others artistically beautiful to match his dreams and nightmares. These images of worship may be ethereal or when brought to literal realities become men writ large or god writ small. Often they are unique men or supermen — the heroes of folklore and legend, the stuff of which Kings are made. The Hero assures safety and fulfills the need for obeisance — the search of the human ego for repose in the person of a larger being an identity reaching beyond the meagre self into a merger with a larger life — a vicarious existence in fantasy where all wishes are realized beyond the dreary and bare fulfillment of the demands of daily existence. To the hero are attributed superior virtues and his exploits become legendary. As a superman akin to the gods if not one of them, this man writ large becomes the sanction for custom (law and order), justice or the apportioning of scarcity to the various orders of men and in the long run the adjuster of social conflicts. However, even heroes are mortal. How can continuity be maintained? Long disputes and even civil wars often develop over the succession. This is truly the thorniest problem of government whether in political democracies, communist dictatorships, or hereditary monarchies. The practice of an hereditary descent from father to son offers a ready made means of maintaining stability and peace. But monarchs are human beings whose weaknesses often make themselves evident especially their desire for the property and women of the tribe. The rape of the Sabine women by imperfect monarchs and the untoward behavior of George III, who was not the last German ruler to be a victim of mental disease — especially afflicted with delusions of grandeur — illustrate the imperfection of hereditary descent. But monarchy has many values. It affords glamour and glory, pomp and ceremony vicariously enjoyed. Under monarchy, there are princes especially charming princes and above all lovely princesses. Princes charming play a significant role not only in the fairy stories of the Grimm brothers but in novels of Victorian writers and of course in the popular art form — the movies. Their appeal is to romantic females comprising now over fifty percent of the electorate. It is now proposed to expand the number of romantics to include girls of eighteen because boys at that age are all old enough to fight, *ergo* their sisters are qualified to vote. The transfer of this popular art form into a political institution is now a regular part of Republican popular government in California.

That Americans were not strangers to the allurement of and even the naturalness of monarchy was attested by the one-third (by John Adam's estimate) who preferred the Tory monarchy in 1775-80 and by those who created a monarchy in miniature around the persons of the colonial governors. In fact, the presidency was created to fit the personality of George Washington, a revolutionary hero and the embodiment of the virtues of the British landed gentry — the colonial squirearchy which has enchanted southern visions from Washington through Robert E. Lee to the vicarious Rhett Butler — Clark Gable of "Gone With The Wind" whose popularity is witnessed by box office receipts even today. What a new face he would have offered in contrast to the plebeian countenances of Hubert Humphrey and Richard Nixon. Franklin Roosevelt's third and fourth terms are other evidence of the longing for royalty and continuity. The discovery of a new royal family — the Kennedys — has found reinforcement from the youth and by their obsequious mentors, alleged liberal intellectuals especially the editors and writers in *Harper's* and the *New Republic*.

A large proportion of human social problems as well as biological ones are insoluble. But hope springs eternal in the electoral psyche. Both wishfully and wistfully man seeks surcease from his increasing unhappiness in the midst of material affluence. Scarcity of necessities and the urge for distinction by means of enjoying luxuries induces social conflict and individual competition so that the group process as often produces chaos as order. This is true of other institutions than political ones. One witnesses the same incessant struggle in religion in a perpetual dialogue too often apt to degenerate into disastrous violence. In Christendom disputes over organization and doctrine led to the primacy of Rome and ultimately to the doctrine of infallibility. In political affairs the desire for peace compels the authoritarian family or no family at all in the chaotic emotions which left undisciplined destroys everything including themselves! But authoritarianism and dynasties as often produce tyranny as peace. For every Richard the Lionhearted, there is a John the jealous hearted, which leads to a covenant — a constitution — and a due process laid down in either prescriptive or written form.

In a new world widely dispersed units of local government supported by a self-sufficing agriculture found little need for establishments either in government or religion. Farmers and plantations governed themselves except when threatened by foreign invasion or security to their land titles — the basis of this isolated society. In trying to create a government sufficient to assure trade, defense, and credit, the Philadelphia framers of 1787 had not only their experience with colonial governors to guide them but their education in the classics with wide-spread and extensive reading in the originals — political experiences of Greece and Rome with institutions of power. Finding it necessary to have some unity since the Revolution had shown the weakness of representative government without a central executive, they sought to avoid the pitfalls of monarchy though some, including Hamilton, found the possibility of continuity small without a dynasty.

FROM THE NEW YORK PACKET, TUESDAY, MARCH 18, 1788
THE FEDERALIST NO. 70
Alexander Hamilton

TO THE PEOPLE OF THE STATE OF NEW YORK:

"There is an idea, which is not without its advocates, that a vigorous Executive is inconsistent with the genius of republican government. The enlightened well-wishers to this species of government must at least hope that the supposition is destitute of foundation; since they can never admit its truth, without at the same time admitting the condemnation of their own principles. Energy in the Executive is a leading character in the definition of good government. It is essential to the protection of the community against foreign attacks; it is not less essential to the steady administration of the laws; to the protection of property against irregular and high-handed combinations which sometime interrupt the ordinary course of justice;

to the security of liberty against the enterprises and assaults of ambition, of faction, and of anarchy. Every man the least conversant in Roman story, knows how often that republic was obliged to take refuge in the absolute power of a single man, under the formidable title of Dictator, as well against the intrigues of ambitious individuals who aspired to the tyranny, and the seditions of whole classes of the community whose conduct threatened the existence of all government, as against the invasion of external enemies who menaced the conquest and destruction of Rome."

They came up with an office to fit the qualities of their presiding officer, George Washington, plantation owner, military hero, and wealthy farmer whose character was modelled after the English landed gentry and shaped by an idealized stereotype of ancient Roman generals, Cincinnatus, in particular. An elective constitutional monarchy one chosen by a college of cardinals without tenure but composed of lawyers, men of commerce and plantation owners selected by the local landed gentry in their legislatures would select an executive to give unity, energy, and a degree of decision to the new government. Federalists vied with one another in finding a suitable title for this first Consul and sought to weave a crown of titular oak leaves for the charismatic Washington and create sufficient court decorum and mystique to awe the great unwashed in the country and the few artisans who dwelt in cities in process of birth. Hamilton and his fellow officers endeavored to create in the veterans of the Revolution a hereditary society, a new governing class, from whom leadership might be chosen. George Washington was naturally the first president of the Cincinnati, and not unexpectedly, Alexander Hamilton was the third. Not surprisingly, Charles Pinckney, the second president of this military elite was Hamilton's choice for Washington's successor rather than John Adams. Civilians — the unheroic Thomas Jefferson and John Adams, the Hubert Humphrey and Richard Nixon of the time — agreed that the Cincinnati was a bad organization so that Washington was discouraged from being active in its membership.

Conservatives ever since have sought to find constitutional monarchs in military heroes such as William Henry Harrison, Zachary Taylor, Winfield Scott, Ulysses S. Grant, and Dwight Eisenhower with interludes of Generals Hayes, Garfield, Arthur, and Benjamin Harrison, with Major McKinley thrown in to be significant symbols. These heroes or hero images personified the contemporary patriotic virtues of simplicity, frugality and conspicuous self-sacrifice to assure the plebeian electorate of their kinship to George Washington and the founding fathers. Behind these symbols, the Thurlow Weeds, Roscoe Conklings and Charlie Wilsons governed in the interest of the dominant economic and industrial forces. The personality quirks, the individual foibles from corncob pipe smoking (W. H. Harrison), horse racing (Grant), dutiful husband (McKinley) and golfing (Eisenhower) were used as opiates for the readers of the penny press and the listeners and viewers of the mass media. A fatherly smile rather than clear syntax and effective advocacy furnished the ablest arguments for public policy or no policy at all.

Nor have liberals been averse to the hero, though they are more likely to envisage him as a reformer carrying out the will of the masses. Andrew Jackson certainly embodied the virtues of a fighting frontiersman and his strong will and ruthless disregard of heretofore accepted protocol made him a hero on the order of Julius Caesar, though he lacked the former's patrician background. He institutionalized mass emotion in his single slogan "Hurrah for Jackson," the short and effective answer to all Whig contentions. He discovered in the interstices of the constitution the power to destroy the U.S. National Bank and master his cabinet. His newspaper propagandists, Kendall and Blair, set patterns for future manipulation of public opinion. Jackson's success was so great that the Whigs emulated the new appeal by nominating Harrison and Taylor rather than Clay or Webster in 1840 and 1848. Politicians such as Van Buren have never been popular. In other words the warrior turned reformer — becomes a *princeps* or leader who molds public policy by control of a party by the manipulation of opinion.

Though without a heroic military record, Abraham Lincoln observed Jackson's success. He sent a memorandum for Zachary Taylor's perusal urging him to dramatize the presidency and take credit for acts performed rather than giving his subordinates the praise. As president forced by circumstances to take unprecedented actions, the rural corporation lawyer found new emergency powers to suspend *habeas corpus* and to confiscate two billion dollars worth of property in the possession of rebels though he much preferred the middle way of compensation. He was a superb wheeler-dealer. At first an artful politician he grew to be much more than *princeps* for he became also *imperator* or commander-in-chief. The *imperium* was conferred upon, or assumed by, the first consul who held office during a time of domestic rebellion. As *imperator* he sought to set up a presidential power to reconstruct the states in rebellion. He was on a collision course with Congress when John Wilkes Booth made him the Supreme Messiah of American nationalism, the one whose deeds had preserved the union and as *princeps* of the Republican Party with a transferable halo put the martyr's mantle upon his party for three score years. The failure of Andrew Johnson as *princeps* destroyed Lincoln's successor as *imperator* and the old Senatorial Cabal seized control behind the heroic mask of a *rex*, U. S. Grant, whose simple acceptance speech was "Let us have peace." Behind Grant, Roscoe Conkling's New York machine held the party under rigid discipline. *Rex* amused himself with horses and alcohol to the consternation of Henry Adams and his aristocratic Bostonian intellectuals while a new governing class of industrialists arose in the economy. These Robber Barons consolidated, centralized and integrated the economy as self-sufficing farmers fought a losing battle in the new market economy, part free and competitive and part slave or monopolistic.

Presidents served little active functions either as *princeps* or as *imperator* from Lincoln until Theodore Roosevelt though Grover Cleveland exercised a mild *rex* power as a vetoer of parliamentary rewards to honest G. A. R. veterans not always heroic. It was Roosevelt the first who tried to exert all the powers of *rex, princeps* and *imperator*. He became the first Caesar who built up a regal court loyal to him, surrounded by obsequious courtiers both political and poetic. The exercise of imperial powers in peace time as well as during an insurrection became a part of the Theodorian regime. Even as Assistant Secretary of the Navy he had issued an executive order to Admiral Dewey designed to involve or provoke war though a timid Methodist *rex* hesitated to use it. Theodore was the first escalator of war. Once president the redoubtable Rough Rider mounted a horse of imperial posture. He not only "took Panama" under his authority as *imperator* or commander-in-chief, but threw his imperial might around the world by sending the fleet to Japan, acting as mediator of the Russo-Japanese War and generally asserted American sovereignty over the Caribbean. Domestically he expounded the legally untenable constitutional doctrine that residual constitutional authority reposed in the executive if not otherwise allocated. He arbitrated labor disputes by presidential prestige. He soon assumed the *principate* by using the appointive power to control the Republican party and renominate himself. He not only reelected himself but determined the succession. His poor judgment in nominating a new 350 pound Caesar who applied only legal powers of policy and legislative action resulted in an attempt to seize the regal power again by challenging Taft's authority as *princeps*. In fact, Roosevelt sought to reestablish himself in the imperial office by an appeal to a party plebiscite. Though personally unsuccessful, he changed the nature of the Republican party as the senatorial cabal which selected Harding did little to conciliate the Roosevelt worshipers.

Woodrow Wilson as a political scientist had once deplored the presidency as a feeble office in the 1880's but afterward studied T. R.'s actions and began to exalt the presidential power to the same autocratic extent that he had attempted to use his powers as president of Princeton. By reading his message in person to Congress he restored the monarchical image of George Washington. In bypassing Congress and going to the electorate with his propaganda he assumed the imperial robes of plebiscitary democracy. Repeatedly he employed his power as *rex* to build up pressure upon an unwilling Congress to enact legislation which as *princeps* of the Democratic party he had advocated in competition with Roosevelt as the leading voice of the populace.

In foreign affairs, Wilson ploughed his own lonely furrow with little or no consultation with the Senate or Congress in setting a policy which involved the United States in World War I and thereafter attempted to establish a world federation to maintain international law and order. His appeal as *princeps* failed because as *imperator* he had travelled abroad and negotiated treaties without maintaining his *princeps* position in his party. He had failed to establish his domestic position as party leader and spokesman for the masses while he embarked upon imperial conquests. Not until Lyndon Johnson was another president to be so radically repudiated by failing to use his *princeps* role to reconcile the disparity between his informal positions as *rex* with his formidable influence as *imperator*.

What Henry Cabot Lodge did to Woodrow Wilson, Eugene McCarthy did to Lyndon Johnson. It remains to be seen whether the United States repeals the Vietnam conflict as it did World War I. Also it will be interesting to see if another Warren G. Harding assumes the *rex* role in the presidency.

Wilson's three Republican successors lapsed into nominal holders of the authority of *rex*. Calvin the Calm succeeded Harding the Handsome. Harding was a preview of the television model of *rex*. Coolidge fortunately never was exposed to the evil eye of the camera and the female electorate had not yet come into its own. Hoover was a civilian hero, the great humanitarian who had fed the hungry, clothed the naked, ministered to the suffering of the sick, and healed the wounds of both widows and orphans. To him the imperial office was one of sentiment and moral admonition but he rejected the hairshirt of *princeps* and cast aside the role of *imperator*. He had made a rash implied promise to perform the miracle of abolishing poverty. In all three roles he failed as economic disaster overwhelmed him.

Hoover's Democratic successor was a remote member of the Republican Roosevelt dynasty but spiritually created in the image of Theodore. The royal purple in all of its shades was tailored to garb this aristocratic pragmatist who enjoyed and was exhilarated by the use of power.

He was the articulate spokesman, the genuine *princeps* of his party which he remodeled into a going concern, a coalition of previously frustrated minorities. The Democratic party changed itself from a faintly baroque organization dominated by the descendants of Confederate army officers intermixed with a residue of bankrupt farmers still lamenting the collapse of populism into an active and vigorous group of amalgamated labor leaders and leftist professional intellectuals. Taking advantage of the technology of radio his eloquent and confident voice acted as a tonic to the helpless and discouraged, whose numbers were greatly enlarged by self-allocation into the descriptive category of forgotten men. Franklin Roosevelt became a virtual Augustus who founded a new *principate* which humbled "the robber barons" whom he dubbed "tories" and "economic royalists." New tools of regulation were established over the business community; though the patricians retained their property they lost some of their prestige. They were made propaganda whipping boys of the Eastern William Jennings Bryan who spoke in Harvard accented tones, and moved in the First Social Circles of the Establishment, presiding over both bread and circuses with a whimsical smile. He smote with might and main the prescriptive constitution framed and enforced by the nine elderly vestal virgins wrapped in the garments known as judicial robes. *Rex* Roosevelt almost fulfilled the prescription for political trinity. He reestablished the authority of the chief executive now well reenforced by an enlarged bureaucracy and richly endowed with delegated powers. Confirmed by an unprecedented plebiscite in 1936, he sought at first unsuccessfully to subdue the Supreme Court but in the long run he reconstituted its personnel from ones whose values were those of stability and continuity into ones whose views favored innovation. The new court finally wrought a legal revolution by including a servile uprising in the form of a Spartacan minister wearing the spiritual garments of Mohandas Gandhi.

However, *imperator* Roosevelt was already confronted by a foreign challenge greater than that which had been faced by any of his predecessors. The very continuance of democracy was at stake as the weapons of the new technology had put into the hands of a mad man undreamed of power to subdue the will to freedom of lesser men. At

first boldly announcing a quarantine of aggressors, Roosevelt was rebuffed by the isolationist sentiments of millions of countrymen whose
nostalgia for the days before 1914 still controlled their thoughts and
deeds. Thwarted in his direct approach as a lion he became a fox who
used his authority as Commander-in-Chief or *imperator* to build up
the navy, the air force, and ultimately to produce conscription in peace
time. Finally, recognizing the human desire for continuity he accepted
a third term and broke tradition to be president for a longer term than
anyone else in American history.

If in 1940, Roosevelt ran as *rex* to preserve peace and security, he
soon became *imperator* as the Japanese attack upon Pearl Harbor
opened up new avenues of power. With the zest of Theodore Roosevelt
and the international outlook of Woodrow Wilson, he became a genuine
lion who roared and clawed as well. Boldly demanding unprecedented
industrial output in weapons he was Commander-in-Chief in a titanic
two front war. Diplomatically the uncrowned Augustus paved the
way for a new collective security drive by joining Churchill in creating
a United Nations informally and setting up the machinery for a future
world organization. Faced with an election during wartime his propaganda campaign emphasized now his roles as *imperator* — the in-
dispensable Commander-in-Chief. Liberals took up the slogan unmind-
ful of his duty as *princeps,* for he had lost complete control of the party
apparatus so that instead of his own personal choice, Henry Wallace,
as his successor, he chose or allowed to be chosen a "throttlebottom"
in the person of Harry S. Truman. Thus the succession fell to a man ill
equipped for the *rex* or *imperator* roles and who was at first uncertain
in his *princeps* function though one of the principal reasons for his
selection was to allow the Senate to play a significant part in the post
war treaty and international organization decisions.

Truman was no *rex,* for instead of allowing his advisors to take the
blame for mistakes he took the fire directly upon himself. In 1950
after reelection as *princeps* he donned imperial robes and entered the
Korean adventure. He had already accepted the challenge of Stalin
to establish a *pax Sovietica* by intervention in Greece and the creation
of the Marshall Plan. In NATO and the Berlin blockade he extended
the *pax Americana* to Berlin and in Korea to the thirty-eighth parallel.
As *imperator* he had developed the tactic of depending upon pro-
consuls from the military establishment with General Marshall handling
diplomacy, General Eisenhower, commander in NATO and Generalis-
simo and Mikado MacArthur in the Asian Theatre. Forced at last to
preserve the civilian facade of the republic, Captain Truman summoned

all of his Missouri courage and militarily retired the one proconsul whose image in his own mind fitted him for the Julius Caesar role. His psychologically effective return threatened the civilian control of policy in the provinces and cast a shadow at home, but fortunately age and the presence of a strong competitor in the heroic Eisenhower, the first and only candidate for president in American history to declare his candidacy on foreign soil, thwarted him.

Since Eisenhower temperamentally was more a co-ordinator than a proconsul, his personality made him more *rex* than *imperator*. His benign, Freudian, paternal smile, his image of virility and his symbolism as a small town Horatio Alger success fitted him as a hero candidate. Though sufficiently an *imperator* to prevent his party from returning to its ancient moorings of economic nationalism he was not a belligerent proconsul. He enjoyed the charismatic role of constitutional monarch who personified all the generally accepted virtues of middle class America. As *princeps* he was a total failure. He did not build his party apparatus at all. He did not formulate any domestic programs or legislation. Instead he left this function to his Vice President. Avoiding any task as innovator, the beloved Ike presided over the cabinet, played golf and expounded a somewhat monarchical propaganda job in a foggy advocacy of peace. As constitutional monarch he allowed his appointees, Dulles in foreign policy, Ezra Taft Benson in agriculture, Charles Wilson in defense and George Humphrey in the Treasury to make policy decisions. Even a *majordomo*, modelled after Charles Martell, performed the ministerial functions in a regal court until acceptance of a gift of a vicuna coat led to his reluctant resignation. The ethic of the hound's tooth destroyed him.

Eisenhower's success as constitutional monarch was aided by a Democratic senator, Lyndon Johnson, who willingly and even anxiously accepted the senatorial mantle of *princeps* after the unfortunate death of *princeps* Robert A. Taft. The two party merger during the Eisenhower years gave the external appearance of peace and security. In fact, hero worship fostered icon worship. One elderly Republican female in Lincoln, Nebraska, placed an Eisenhower statue in a hallowed cubicle of her comfortable residence similar to alcoves reserved for the virgin in the homes of the faithful in south European countries. Had not the Republican amendment placed in the constitution at the behest of Roosevelt haters, both Republicans and southern Democrats, prohibited a third term, the constitutional monarchy under Eisenhower would have continued indefinitely, even though we fell behind the Russians in outer space and weaponry and continued disastrous farm policies. The Vice President, Richard Nixon had so entrenched himself in party circles as Republican *princeps* that he assured his nomination over the challenge of the Rockefeller millions. His well advertised experience plus traditional religious objections to a Catholic monarch almost made him president. However, Senator John Kennedy sensed a growing desire for a *princeps* with dynamic policies and a general movement forward instead of a glorification of the *status quo*.

Young Kennedy had not lived in Great Britain during his father's incumbency at the court of St. James for nothing. He had likewise studied the rise to power of Hitler in Germany. After a photogenic triumph in his defeat in the 1956 Democratic convention he became the popular symbol of youth, wealth, culture and of persecuted minorities (a Catholic victim of bigotry) but even more he was a war hero whose escape from patriotic martyrdom was nearly miraculous. Additionally, he was a victim of a physical ailment almost fatal which attracted attention of those seeking a vicarious Messiah similar to the brave but crippled Roosevelt. Finally, Kennedy was urbane, witty, and articulate; he had written a best seller book analyzing the virtues of courage in politics. As a political Lochinvar in glamorous garb, he barely won election, but at inauguration and afterward he assumed the leadership of a post war generation, surrounded himself with a cultural entourage of literate admirers. Thereby John Kennedy created a style not seen in the White House since Theodore Roosevelt's day. His regal dignity epitomized the legend that the lace curtain Irish fresh from the rituals of Harvard could don the royal purple as well as the imperial Dutch Roosevelts of New York similarly educated in America's most snobbish intellectual training ground for a governing class.

His charming little Irish daughter, Caroline, soon melted the cold and bigoted hearts of Protestant mothers and touched the stony sentiments of more than a few fathers. His wife filled the delicate role of First Lady in a French and Hollywood style of royalty by her ultra refined image of a princess in the ermine. Soon the Kennedys were performing excellently in the monarchical role of *rex* and appeared on their way to creating a dynasty with an abundance of not too modest fraternal ambitions. Linked by electoral accident to the lowest minority in the hierarchy, the hapless descendants of former slaves, the Kennedys not only appeared to be a reincarnation of the Gracchi brothers but even the leaders of a Spartacus revolution. The Bay of Pigs fiasco tarnished the *imperator* image gravely but was retrieved in a trial of wills in the Cuban missile crisis.

As *princeps*, Kennedy failed to get the support of the Senate as his reform legislation was stalled in congressional committee where the youthful chief executive seemed loath to put his popular prestige on the line. He displayed Theodore Rooseveltian dash and vigor in temporarily subduing an uprising of steel barons by his effort to maintain an even price level in 1962. Though an open advocate of the Keynesian doctrines of economic growth by fiscal manipulation, the President was balked by a stubborn Congress reluctant to depart from the hoary balanced budget theory of government. Civil rights legislation had no greater success with the senatorial coalition of southern Democrats and midwestern Republican conservatives firmly in charge of the congressional machinery. *Princeps* Lyndon Johnson had been turned into a "throttlebottom" by the camp followers in the Kennedy entourage so he could no longer wave his magic wand over a compliant Senate. Kennedy had opened the Pandora's box of mob action by inviting the public demonstration by the minority in 1963.

Fearful tragedy intervened and Camelot fell at the hands of a deranged assassin. Court life in the fairy land White House suddenly ended both for Caroline and Arthur Schlesinger. A Texas outlander was president. A new test of the presidency was at hand. For the first time in history a powerful senator only recently majority leader had become Chief Executive. The dream denied to Webster, Calhoun and Clay, to Benton and to Blaine, as well as to La Follette and to Robert A. Taft, was now the reality of Lyndon B. Johnson.

At first he fulfilled the *rex* role to perfection. As the nation's monarch in mourning, with tact and good taste he performed the first task of an heir unexpectedly called to the throne—continuity. "Let us continue," he solemnly declared and the nation heaved a sigh of relief. Gathering in his hands all of the threads of authority in the *imperium* he asserted the full powers of a *princeps* and *rex*. He succeeded in breaking the congressional log jam. First to give way was the powerful baron from Virginia, Harry S. Byrd, Sr., who yielded to the principate. The economics of Keynes was accepted as a tax cut was enacted enlarging an existing deficit in order to permit a cut in unemployment, the gnawing problem of the new industrial state. A plunge into unprecedented prosperity followed with a real economy of technological abundance and material affluence. The commitment of the dead president to pass a civil rights act as a step in the liquidation of three hundred years of slavery was fulfilled by the skillful use of cloture, thus wrecking the long time southern veto of the legislative process. A delicate reconciliation of the church and state conflict paved the way for the passage of substantial federal aid to education. The tools of the party were centralized in executive hands and renomination and reelection became a foregone conclusion.

However, *princeps* Johnson did not absorb the heir apparent of the Kennedy dynasty into the vice presidency. He failed to maintain the order of succession for the newly discovered dynasty. He had woefully offended not only the dynastic heirs but even more their liberal sycophants in the press and what by some strange irony is referred to as the intellectual community. *Princeps* Johnson had likewise led two Minnesota senators up on the mountain. He chose the cherub instead of the lean and hungry, poetry loving Cassius who maintained a political vendetta against both the living and the dead Caesar. There is no wrath like that of a political professor scorned.

Princeps Johnson's Republican opposition suddenly was seized by a peculiar virus, a nostalgia for the good old days preceding Franklin Roosevelt. They chose to run the race of 1936 over again with easily predictable results. To establish a two party system in the south, they surrendered their hegemony in the north. The Johnson-Humphrey landslide equalled or surpassed the Roosevelt 1936 avalanche. In full control of both houses of Congress the *principate* successfully passed more domestic reforms than any other administration in history. The Great Society was in full bloom. The promise to end poverty had been an unnecessary embellishment of campaign oratory — in a sense a warmover of Herbert Hoover's Messiah campaign of 1928.

Neither Julius nor Augustus Caesar, not even Marcus Aurelius, had to confront television. The Roman imperial front did not depend upon images nor photogenic talents. Neither did the Roman *princeps* need to suffer the criticisms of journalists with Messiah complexes. Rome had the censorate but their judgments came at the end of the consular term. The censors did not try to substitute their omniscience for the judgment of officials. Roman officials confronted only those in the forum not an electorate of more than one hundred million. The lens of the censors was now as powerful as the pen and mightier than the sword.

The royal diadem did not include the Harvard physiognomy nor did the Texas dialect or idiom, or parables, match those of Boston and Cambridge. Despite dutiful efforts the Johnson family could not equal the sophisticated and snob appeal to the masses of his predecessor's leisure class immediate family. The furrowed Johnson brow did not reflect the sovereign all encompassing smile of the genial but sometimes confused Ike. The Washington correspondents male and female thwarted in obtaining their customary leaks from inside sources began catty comments about the man in the White House, his person, his alleged obscene language and off color metaphors. His personal habits more heavily resembled those of a cowboy than those of the wearer of a crown. Instead of a cult of personality loyalty an epidemic of scapegoatism not evident since Herbert Hoover's day ensued.

Johnson confronted an imperial decision. His role as *imperator* challenged him. His Democratic predecessor Truman had met the *pax Sovietica* threat in Korea through the United Nations. Now that body was a shambles as a result of too many miniature nations, unstable at home and abroad in control of the Assembly with Russia using the veto power in the Council. China threatened to set up a *pax Siniaca* in the Far East. Haunted by the memory of the charge of treason hurled by frustrated Republicans in 1952 after China had fallen into Marxist hands just as the Eisenhower administration had been with respect to Guatemala and as Kennedy had responded with a threat of force in the Cuban missile crisis, Lyndon Johnson as *imperator* faced a baffling decision. He turned to his enormous diplomatic and military bureaucracies for counsel as well as to the burgeoning secret police, the C. I. A.

To allow Vietnam to fall to the Marxists was to be entrapped as the Democrats Truman and Acheson had been after the triumph of Mao Tse Tung in 1949. To embark upon escalation was to risk frustration and entanglement in guerrilla warfare. He seized the latter horn of a dilemma. He undertook as *imperator* to build up American defenses in Asia and simultaneously to maintain the war to end poverty at home. Costs mounted. There was no British sense of duty or Roman instinct of patriotism in American citizens to sustain his endeavors. The corrosive logic of existentialism and latter day Epicureanism flowed from Europe into United States intellectual channels. "A better Red than dead" virus infected many urban youth as agrarian discipline declined. Youthful mobs sought to satisfy their exhibitionist impulses before that marvel of technology, the television camera.

A war without censorship is fought before cameras which focus upon the horrors of one side only. The administration was caught in the quicksands of Asiatic politics where the simple western cultural democratic tools of elections had no deep roots. One civil war had succeeded another and one faction followed still another. Every form of corruption invented in 5,000 years of history still prevailed in a society of Darwinian and Hobbesian characteristics. Anarchy was the host and chaos the outcome of a quarter century of endless violence. *Imperator* Johnson tried valiantly to sustain what his predecessors had started, but now found himself in a quagmire of public despair, confusion, and futility. Promised too much, the city poor and ethnic minorities who had congregated in the slums as a solution to the tenant and agrarian poverty of the 1930's saw on television the kind of life which they regard as typical of the new affluence. The Puritan ethic of work now ridiculed by cynical intellectuals results in a circle of anarchy and nihilism.

In the midst of this turmoil, frustration despite prosperity leads to one of the most primitive of reactions. In prehistoric and even in historic times when panic came after crops failed, or a drought ensued, or a flood occurred, the ruler, king, *rex* or *princeps* was often sacrificed to appease the multitude. Sometimes there was a resort to cannibalism. At other times only blood was offered to appease the wrath of the gods. A harried president, tortured by public opinion polls, lacerated by irate columnists, challenged by erstwhile senatorial colleagues and rejected by would-be vice presidents in 1964, was the target of all of those who wished openly to throw darts and arrows at the wounded gladiator. The lean and hungry Cassius from Minnesota led the charge and when the electorate responded, Brutus, the heir apparent joined the fray. He aroused the emotions of the mob. Here he found another psychopath to whose madness his life became a sacrifice. Felled as *imperator,* tarnished as *rex* and no longer unchallenged as *princeps,* the consensus choice of 1964 became the vicarious sacrifice of 1968. In Buddhist fashion he immolated himself politically. He was consumed by the flames touched off by the censorate and factionalism in his own party.

Can the office of president survive? Is it, like the doctrine of separation of powers, doomed, impaled upon the theology of the trinity? Can anyone less versatile than a combination of Jesus Christ and Julius Caesar with parts of Napoleon added successfully fill an office with standards requiring the talents of a *rex,* a *princeps* and an *imperator* united in one and perform tasks requiring not only charismatic but even divine powers? In an age when God has been assassinated by evangelical theologians, when the authority of the Holy Father is challenged by combinations of the priesthood in the Roman Catholic Church, the survival or *ordo* at the base of civilization itself is at stake. When does pluralism degenerate into anarchism and existential ethics into nihilism? Do the paths of glory through threatened assassination lead only to the grave and oblivion? Is the byproduct of abundance and technological progress the growth of mass psychosis and personal psychopathology?

In the absence of international collective security, what but the *pax Americana* can preserve the semblance of *ordo* and *pax* in a confrontation with *pax sovietica* and *pax Siniaca?* Can the American president be a domestic *princeps* and a foreign *imperator* simultaneously? How can any president perform these diverse tasks and still maintain his healing role as a ceremonial chief and a human god? Must the duties of *pontifex maximus* be added to the trinity? This appeared to be the office George Romney sought before his brains went to the laundry. A new cosmopolitanism demands a god who embraces all the divergent beliefs of a world of many primitive gods suddenly made one by technology but not in spirit. Any *princeps* who can arrange peace for this first generation born into atomic fissions will be a *deus* to the youthful multitude. We have liquidated our agrarian tradition and have nothing to substitute for it. Neither Holy Hubert nor Righteous Richard have the qualifications of Caesar *deus* or even Augustus *divus*.

The photographic lens in its eagerness to furnish conflict and violence to its television viewers whose appetites have been steadily whetted for such fare, has destroyed the nominating convention. Those who consult the popular auspices find more than four of each five voters favoring a primary to select nominees. This will mean a plebiscite every four years. Since the nomination of candidates is the principal function of political parties their demise can easily be foreseen. The death of parties will destroy the chief cohesive force between legislature and executive with potential assassination a hazard to the Estes Kefauver-Eugene McCarthy path to the White House. The television camera becomes the most likely substitute. With no party organization to bolster him in power, a future president will dare not do anything that is not popular whether wise or not. The people of the United States may find themselves in the prospectively happy position of the state of Nebraska with no taxes at all with each form of taxation cut down consecutively by popular referenda. With no test but what the camera reveals, President Hubert Humphrey dare not risk unpopular acts lest he fall before the heir apparent, Teddy Kennedy with his millions, and 22 per cent of the voters favoring his nomination. President Richard Nixon if not confronted with a Rockefeller will have Mayor Lindsay looking over his left shoulder and the hero of Death Valley, Governor Ronald Reagan, peering critically over his right shoulder.

No longer Republicans and Democrats, we will become Reaganista or Kennedyista as the cult of personality so successful in Latin American democracy succeeds our stodgy and unattractive parties. We will await only a DeGaulle to offer us a "yes or no" plebiscite. Limited to two terms by constitutional amendment the president may now be confined to one by the prescriptive and proscriptive character of the independent and frequently irresponsible media. Their survival depends upon selling images, deceptions in the form of advertising. Perhaps some form of dyarchy will be essential as Disraeli created it for the British empire to separate the ceremonial and operating portions of the lofty office.

Some new faith must be substituted for a forgotten agrarian patriotism. The Stoic beliefs of Marcus Aurelius have only a limited appeal in the absence of a dedicated governing class devoted to duty and not concerned only with a confused and confusing bundle of rights. In the absence of a Stoic tradition in our governing class what gives stability to the emotions of a younger generation undisciplined by penury and the handicaps of nature? There are too few Spartan mothers such as Mrs. Rose Kennedy and Mrs. Eleanor Roosevelt. Some new faith must be found to hold together two hundred million people trying to operate political institutions created to bind an allegiance of thirteen agrarian colonies into a single nation.

II

DOES CAMPAIGN SPEAKING
DO GOOD OR HARM?

by

HAROLD F. HARDING

The University of Texas at El Paso

April, 1968

A PROFESSOR OF RHETORIC *addresses himself to the principal query that arises for him from the presidential election. Too little attention of writers on presidential compaigning is devoted to questions relating to speaking. In the past, some speeches have had a profound impact on campaigns — such, for example, as John Kennedy's 1960 speech in Houston to the Protestant ministers on the issue of a Catholic in the White House. Most voter decisions are made on considerations other than rational analysis. The candidate faces many kinds of audiences. Furthermore, the candidate's personality and strengths will have impact upon the manner of his speaking.*

"Does campaign speaking do good or harm?" The weasling answer must be, "It all depends." Our history shows that it is quite possible for mediocre men to attain the presidency. One way to insure a higher average of competence among presidents would be to demand more rational speech from candidates.

● AFTER ALL THE SURPRISES already sprung in the 1968 Presidential Campaign it takes a brash man to make a stand on any statement about candidates or issues, probabilities or possibilities between now and November 5.

The fact that we know so little about how a voter makes up his mind to vote explains in part our doubts about the values of campaign speaking. When I suggested my topic to our chairman this morning he kindly offered a third possibility. He said to me: "Or is it just a waste of time?" You may think it is a waste of time to lifelong, hard-core party members who have voted straight tickets for years. But they need to be reassured. They want to see and hear the man of their choice.

Certainly the personal appearances of the presidential candidates probably have little effect on the hard-core members of the opposition party. It is difficult to conceive of a Goldwater Republican (and there are still millions of them) voting for any Liberal Democrat. Likewise, it is hard to imagine a Liberal Republican voting for any Conservative Democrat.

        ❋   ❋   ❋   ❋

There are many "experts" on the American voter and how he will react in 1968. It is easy to get a long-winded opinion from your barber, your hairdresser, or your bartender. It is easy, too, to get loyal party workers to express their views.

But these are amateur analysts. For many years now the professional opinion analysts of the Inter-University Consortium on Political Research at the University of Michigan have been collecting before and after election samples of opinion.

For reasons not easy to understand political analysts have almost completely disregarded the problem of the *effects* of campaign speaking on voters. The University of Michigan researchers Campbell, Converse, Miller, and Stokes have ignored the matter in their books, *The American Voter* (1960) and *Elections and the Political Order* (1966). Writers like Theodore White, V. O. Key, Milton Cummings, and Samuel Lubell have made only passing references or sketchy ones at best. Our speaker yesterday afternoon, Stanley Kelley, to be sure, has written a book on *Political Campaigning*. I would hope he will comment on the subject later.

Of course, it is possible to dig out comments on the effects of famous campaign speeches — like the FDR Fala speech to the Teamsters and Richard Nixon's defense of his dog, Checkers, and his wife Pat's cloth coat. We do have considerable material about the Kennedy-Nixon "debates" of 1960. But these "debates" are unique in presidential campaigns. There was little critical examining of what Goldwater and Johnson said in 1964 and even less about the direct effects of their speeches on voters. Even now in 1968 we cannot be sure that Eugene McCarthy's success in New Hampshire and Wisconsin was because of his speeches or in spite of them. He is not exactly an orator, you know. Writers have mentioned a variety of reasons for McCarthy's vote, the enthusiasm of his college supporters, his opposition to the war in Vietnam, and the idea that a vote for him is a protest against LBJ.

Why is it that when one consults the index of a scholarly study or even a popular account of presidential elections he seldom finds entries under Speeches, Television Appearances, or Voter Reaction to Campaign Speaking? I ask you to ponder this question during my talk.

I have urged the long-time professional researchers at Ann Arbor to include some questions on speaking in their 1968 study of voting behavior. If the three questions I have suggested are used, we may know a little more from a small sample of voters. But, whatever they say, we must interpret their opinions as of the date given and not as of election day.

* * * *

To go again from the general to the specific we can all think of a few speeches that may have changed some votes. For example, John Kennedy's speech to the Houston ministers in 1960, General Eisenhower's statement in 1952 that if elected, he would go to Korea, and LBJ's dove-like speeches in the fall of 1964, about going easy in Vietnam, in contrast to the frightening, hawk-like speeches of Barry Goldwater.

But the fact remains we have little hard evidence about the effect of the ideas of any speeches. Indeed, if you were to ask even intelligent voters to recall now the positions taken by Johnson and Goldwater on the issues of the 1964 campaign, I think you would find most persons having some trouble remembering just what the stands were, and most persons would have trouble in recalling more than one or two issues. The reason is that in 1964 Goldwater was himself the principal issue. You were either *for* or *against* the man. Johnson made the most of the *Goldwater* issue.

This leads me to assert that, given the widespread use of television in political campaigning, it is the personality of the candidate that counts. I mean his appearance. It is what the public thinks about the candidate's looks rather than his stated positions that counts. Getting well-typed as a good guy is the objective; getting a bad five-o'clock shadow image can be fatal.

The creating of just the right image probably rests on what the public relations man advises more than on what the candidate says in his longer speeches. Of course, a phrase or a sentence from a speech that may be easily remembered can have lasting effect. Goldwater's words about extremism in 1964 and Governor Romney's remarks about being brainwashed in 1968 undoubtedly cost them voter-support.

Here are some hypotheses to remember about the speaker and the speaking situation and the speech itself:

1. The average American voter does not follow all the major candidates in a campaign speaking tour. He is lucky to hear one or two speeches in entirety and then only snatches of others. He may hear something in the form of a television commercial, something, I repeat. It will

be certain short excerpts replayed over and over. He usually listens to the man he prefers rather than to the men he dislikes.

2. The intelligence and educational level of the average voter (tenth grade or less) is such that he cannot follow a complicated chain of argument.

3. Most voters are interested in only one or two of the possible turning points — e.g., the Stand on Vietnam, Civil Rights, Social Security Benefits, or Increased Taxes.

4. The candidate who believes in the hand-shaking, "press the flesh" type of campaign seldom makes any significant policy statements except when he is before a national television network.

5. Most voters judge candidates by their quick-wittedness, humor, good appearance, or attitude toward the audience rather than by their ability to analyze issues, give evidence, or reveal good rhetorical style. Delivery (voice and gesture) is probably more important than invention.

6. An audience likes to be recognized and to have its needs pointed out. Goldwater ignored this precept when he talked against the Tennessee Valley Authority in that region and against features of social security when he spoke to older voters in Florida in 1964.

7. The candidate who speaks to a general audience of young, middle-aged, and old has a most difficult task to please all three groups. If he emphasizes his appeal to one, he offends another. If he ignores one group his interest factor drops. Robert Kennedy and Eugene McCarthy, for example, appeal largely to those under thirty. Richard Nixon probably appeals mostly to the middle-aged conservatives. But Kennedy has recently discovered that there are persons over thirty, and he wants to appeal now to them. George Wallace probably appeals mostly to the less well-educated and the anti-blacks in the backward areas. But there are signs that Wallace's support is widening. Hubert Humphrey is the one man who, by education, experience, and personality, has the capability of making a wide appeal to those between twenty-one and eighty-one.

❖   ❖   ❖   ❖

The best detailed account of presidential campaigns is to be found in the two volumes (1960 and 1964) by Theodore H. White on *The Making of the President.* Of the two, the 1960 volume on Kennedy and Nixon is far better for those who believe that campaign speaking does some good. Perhaps this is because Kennedy did so well in the television debates. Perhaps it is also because the worship of personality and charm had a better actor that year.

On the other hand, if you wish to read about the ineptitude of speakers and the harm they may do to their cause, consult the 1964 volume and study what Goldwater and Miller said to audiences that year. They both became highly skilled at chasing Republicans to the Democratic side.

If you want to examine the art of persuasion before a hostile audience, read John F. Kennedy's speech to the Greater Houston Ministerial Association on September 12, 1960, in the appendix of White's 1960 volume. He describes the audience reaction during and after the speech and makes crystal clear how Kennedy won over an unfriendly group, largely by his candid answers to questions. "When he had finished," White reports, "he had not only closed Round One of his election campaign — he had for the first time more fully and explicitly than any other thinker of his faith defined the personal doctrine of a modern Catholic in a democratic society."[1]

White defines in a brilliant analysis of those who heard JFK in 1960 the kinds of people who attend a political speech, or at least some of Kennedy's speeches in 1960:

The first of the audiences, in size, is always the national audience. Two score newspapermen and reporters of the great national news media follow doggedly in his wake day after day. . . . Not for days or weeks will the candidate know the effect of any speech or statement on the national mood or on the minority group to which it is specifically addressed.

There follows the second audience, the strategically calculated audience. The candidate has picked out individual states, counted their electoral votes, and now he works them one by one. . . . Impact has been made on the state directly; the leading local dignitaries have been met and ignited; the volunteer organizations have assembled and have been tuned up, their enthusiasm at this personal visit must now spread and kindle others.

Then comes the personal audience, so small in numbers as to be minuscule — yet more important than any other. These are the men in work shirts and sport shirts, the women in house dresses with babies in arms, the farmers observing silently, the students listening intently, the bobby-soxers yipping and squealing. These are the people who gather at whistle stops, at airports, at crossroads, in numbers so tiny that there is no point in expending the effort of formal speech writing or policy-making to capture their

[1] Theodore H. White, *The Making of the President 1960* (New York: Atheneum Publishers, 1964), pp. 261-262.

attention. But these are the people who count most. . . . Becoming
President is an utterly personal business between the man who
offers himself as national leader and the Americans who judge him.
The candidate must feel the beat of the people he hopes to lead;
their heart is his target. And no public-opinion poll or analysis can
tell him half so well whether he has reached that target as can the
people themselves, giving him the beat of their response.[2]

✿   ✿   ✿   ✿

What is likely to be the cast of the *speaking* of the candidates now on
the horizon for the 1968 Election? Will it do good or harm? I define
"good" to mean bringing in votes and "harm" to mean scaring them
away.

Well, there are George Wallace, Eugene McCarthy, Robert Kennedy,
Richard Nixon and probably Hubert Humphrey and perhaps Ronald
Reagan and Governor Rockefeller to consider as of now. Let us take
them in that order.

Let no one discount the effect of George Wallace's speaking in 1968.
You may deplore his ideas, his style, and his strategy. But never underestimate the man. He makes an appeal to more Americans than are
willing to admit the fact. If we have more riots in the cities this summer
and if there is a violent demonstration at the Chicago Convention, the
enthusiasm for Wallace is bound to leap up. You may interpret it not
as a protest to the failure of the other parties but as a genuine endorse-
ment of all that George Wallace stands for. If ever there was an example
of the need for studying rhetorical theory, just to protect yourself and
to defend your good judgment, here is the man who best typifies the
need. Millions of persons in the lowest educational levels will listen to
Wallace, join his cause, and vote for him. His influence extends far
beyond the Southern States. His voice is heard in all fifty states. Here
is how Ray Jenkins explains Wallace's tactics:

> To get maximum exposure Wallace schedules as many press
> conferences and television interviews as possible between rallies.
> These exchanges rarely develop any new information, but Wallace
> relishes the battle of wits and usually comes out on top. . . . If all
> else fails, Wallace will treat the '68 race as a warm-up for '72.[3]

I believe that much of Wallace's appeal rests upon his constant
belittling of what he calls the pseudo-intellectuals, meaning anyone
with more than a high school education. He baits his opposition by

2 *Ibid.*, pp. 254-255.

3 Ray Jenkins, "George Wallace Figures to Win Even If He Loses," *New York Times Magazine*, April 7, 1968, pp. 75-76.

the boast that he is a former truck driver and his wife a former dime store clerk. This is amusing until we realize that there are several million truck drivers and dime store clerks in our country, some of whom do not need learned speeches to identify with Wallace, and to vote for him. He makes people believe in what he says. Is this a good or a harm?

Senator McCarthy will probably not get the Democratic nomination at Chicago. But between now and then he can make many speeches, do some harm to other candidates, and do some good for himself. I doubt that he can ever attract the widest following. The sides on the issues he has chosen are not the most popular. He opposes the War in Vietnam, he favors a guaranteed annual wage, and he seeks a still better form of medical insurance for the poor. These are significant issues, and Senator McCarthy can expect to attract a hearing on them from the better educated of our citizens. He is the nearest in type to Adlai Stevenson among the present crop and he will attract a thoughtful following.

Robert Kennedy's speeches will be designed to harm others and to steal the show for himself. He will be thoroughly opposed to the Johnson-Humphrey administration. If Humphrey runs *he* will be Bobby Kennedy's main issue. We may expect the same kind of campaign we witnessed in the Humphrey-Nixon West Virginia primary in 1960, except on a greatly enlarged scale. It will be a case of character assassination all over again. With speech writers like Ted Sorenson, Richard Goodwin, and Adam Walinsky available, there should be no shortage of statements and press releases. But Kennedy's blitzkrieg tactics have sometimes backfired on him, as they did when he attacked Senator Javits of New York. Of one thing we can be sure, the Kennedy organization will win when newspaper and television coverage are measured. There will be front-page material available every day if editors and program directors will only present or publish it.

What about Hubert Humphrey? He is a good speaker, probably the best of the lot. But his devotion to LBJ has cost him some support from Liberal Democrats and especially the Americans for Democratic Action, now committed to Senator McCarthy. Humphrey will inherit the Johnson support and in a sense has a ready-made organization standing by. He has the energy, the charm, and charisma of a sort. He is too old and a bit too tarnished to appeal to the present generation of college students. But high-class debating skill may bring Humphrey up in the Gallup and Roper polls. In a debate between Bobby and Hubert, I would not risk a large bet on Bobby this time. He is too sullen, too surly, and too moody to come over well on television. Humphrey's humor and sharp replies will give him extra points.

But in the final analysis let us remember that money talks. The way the Kennedy machine under Pierre Salinger has been buying up television time in Nebraska is indicative of the strategy to come. The pressure put on Larry O'Brien to head up the Kennedy campaign was tremendous. He is supposed to want to be loyal to LBJ and Hubert Humphrey, but he has abandoned them after the heat was put on. The Irish Mafia does not easily forget or forgive. O'Brien has apparently been *scared* into his new job with a knife at his back.

I should say something about Richard Nixon and Governors Rockefeller and Reagan. They are all good performers, and it is probably too early to think that Nixon has the nomination sewed up. There will be lots of threats, bargains, trades, and sell-outs before the third ballot at Miami Beach. To me the most appealing and best qualified of the three is Rockefeller. Nixon may be the better speaker and Reagan may have a better image, especially among the Goldwater Republicans, but there are bound to be a few more surprises in the coming months. Again, remember that money talks.

Nixon is supposed to have mellowed and improved. Reagan is supposed to have matured. As speakers I distrust both of them. If the war in Vietnam drags on and Robert Kennedy is the Democratic candidate, I would prefer to see Rockefeller running against him.

* * * *

Does campaign speaking do good or harm? Or is it just a waste of time? The only expert who can answer these questions is the voter himself — you, the first-time voter, or you, the old hand who has heard the promises of many campaigns.

There is no simple, easy answer. Our political history is replete with examples that support each side, for good or harm. Extensive campaign speaking in many places, as we know it, is a relatively modern part of the electoral process, not much more than forty years old. I heard the 1924 Democratic Convention by radio while in college. Al Smith spoke over the radio in 1928. FDR perfected his national speaking style in 1932 and later. It was Harry Truman's whistle-stop campaign that turned the tide against Dewey in 1948. It is true that television came into wide political use in the 1950's, but it was the 1960 Kennedy-Nixon campaign where the full force of television speaking was strongly felt.

I could easily list more examples to show how votes were *probably* lost by poor speaking or *possibly* won over by good speaking. But my opinions would be guesses. Even in this electronic age we have no complete set of after-action reports telling just how and why a voter reached his decision. Could you believe the voter even if he did make his statement after voting? I doubt it. The way a man may vote, I believe, defies collective analysis. It can be a combination of so many factors. So often it is just a form of protest-voting against the past administration, the establishment, or the local machine. Or again, in places where machine control may still exist the voter may simply be doing what he is told to do. A further complicating factor is the fact that nowadays about a third of all voters label themselves independents. True, they may have leanings to one of the old line parties. But the fact that they say they are undecided or independent probably means that they are ticket-splitters or just plain "wait-and-see-ers." In many a close election the independents determine the outcome. We have almost learned to distrust all polls made a month before election day or even a week before election day. This year the race may be so close I advise you to hedge your bets. In 1968 it is entirely possible for us to elect a "minority" president, a man who has not received a majority of the popular vote.

If I seem to be avoiding a clear-cut judgment, I have to confess that my answer to the question, "Does Campaign Speaking do Good or Harm?" is simply a weasling, "It all depends." It depends on you, the voter. Because different speakers affect different hearers in different ways, you may detest Richard Nixon or Robert Kennedy but the persons sitting on either side of you may consider each a hero — absolutely the best man for the presidency.

This is because we are all affected by our emotions, our family political traditions, our long-standing dislikes. Samuel Lubell's book *The Future of American Politics,* is sprinkled with quotations from life-long Republicans who "are not going to change now," or disgruntled ones saying just the opposite. It is a mistake to think that there is no rhyme or reason to the way a voter makes up his mind. There is, but nobody has explained it. We ought to know by now that elections are full of surprises, of upsets, of inexplicable factors.

The studies show that there are stable, consistent voters and fickle, party-hopping voters. Alienation from a party is a far more common disease now than in my boyhood. Speeches may be a cause of this disease. Nowadays, voters openly boast that they will cross over, and in some of our states we seek to facilitate such action in the primary elections. Party registration no longer means a life commitment.

Perhaps the greatest single factor in the unpredictability of elections nowadays is the impact of a new crisis just before an election. One such crisis would be that we could completely end the war in Vietnam before November. Others might be that we would be forced off the gold standard; or that we would begin a nuclear exchange with the USSR; or that the Chinese Communists would attack India; or that the Soviet submarine fleet would challenge our fleet in the Mediterranean; or that we would meet unexpected reverses in Southeast Asia; or that the President might be assassinated. These are not wild ideas. They are all in the realm of possibility. Any one of these eventualities could persuade a voter to change his mind.

✿   ✿   ✿   ✿

McGeorge Bundy, president of the Ford Foundation and former special Assistant to Presidents Kennedy and Johnson, made some far-ranging suggestions in the Godkin lectures he delivered recently at Harvard. He urged that we upgrade our concepts about the Presidency and those who assist in that office. We need, he said, "A new level of support for strong government." He meant strong government for freedom and then he added, "I emphatically include the general idea that one great part of freedom is to have a part in your own government, especially when it affects you directly."

Where can participation and direct effect mean more than in the educational process of selecting the best qualified person for the office of the Presidency? Voters must take this obligation far more seriously than in the past. They need to study the requirements of the office, the qualifications of the candidates, and then they must estimate the capacity of each for growth on the job.

Over the nearly two hundred years of our history we have had some remarkable men as presidents. We have also had some remarkably ill-suited men in the office. Part of this latter fact can be attributed to the system by which we nominate and elect men for this highest office. This system has many flaws, and 1968 will probably highlight them, if a large vote for George Wallace throws the election into the House of Representatives. Alexander Hamilton wrote:

> The process of election affords a moral certainty that the office of President shall never fall to the lot of any man who is not in an eminent degree endowed with the requisite qualifications. . . . It will not be too strong to say that there will be a constant probability of seeing the station filled by characters pre-eminent for ability and virtue.[4]

4 *The Federalist*, No. 68.

I ask you to run over the list of our presidents and ponder the wisdom of Hamilton's forecast. How many of the men like Wallace, Kennedy, McCarthy, Humphrey, Nixon, Reagan, and Rockefeller are "pre-eminent for ability and virtue"?

Perhaps some of our trouble comes from the man seeking the office. We have had few cases like that of Adlai Stevenson, where the office sought the man. When I think of the ruthlessness of Robert Kennedy in seeking the Presidency as if he were sole lawful heir, I am reminded of a sentence in one of Thomas Jefferson's letters: "Whenever a man has cast his longing eyes on them [high public offices] a rottenness begins in his conduct."[5] The Robert Kennedy campaign of the next few months, at least until the Chicago convention, may prove the long-range foresight of Jefferson's dictum.

* * * * *

I like to think that conditions are changing and that voters today are more concerned, better informed, and more active participants than ever before. I hope that the role played by college students in Senator McCarthy's campaign in New Hampshire, Wisconsin, and Indiana has great portent for the future. These young voters or potential voters are creating a current that is bound to be felt beyond 1968. They will not be satisfied with the old-fashioned ballyhoo of political campaigns. They want explanations. They demand definite stands on issues. They are finding out the shortcomings and inadequacies of older citizens as voters who too often cast ballots without good reasons. In short, the traditions of the old parties may be tested and shaken in 1968 as never before.

But, unless we can arrange a series of well-planned television debates (not question shows) among the top four candidates in October, 1968, I do not see much prospect of getting a higher intellectual content in the campaign. When we consider the millions of dollars spent by the advertising agencies and public relations firms to project an image for their man, it is a pity that a small portion cannot be used to let the candidate tell us where he stands, to let him answer voters' questions, and to refute his opponent on issues. I believe that college-educated persons must demand a better deal this year. In the words of Adlai Stevenson: "Egg-heads of the world unite! You have only your yolks to lose."

And so I plead again for a better understanding by voters of the

5 Letter to Tench Coxe, 1799.

process of electing the president. I warn that it is a long and rigorous labor to follow what the candidates say and do from the conventions to election day. This year it is even harder because the campaign really began a year ago. If LBJ had decided to become a candidate I would say it began the day after the 1964 election.

It is not enough to go to the polling place next November 5 and pull the straight-ticket lever. The process of choice requires reading, reflection, a making of constant comparisons, a study of our world and domestic situations, and finally a narrowing down to the one man who can best do the job that has to be done. John F. Kennedy expressed the idea well in a Los Angeles speech in September, 1960, when he said: "All of you will in a sense, in 1961, hold office in the Great Republic; upon all of you in your own way and in your own life great responsibilities will be placed."[6]

Americans unfortunately are too often impressed by price tags — I mean high price tags. But if every voter could be brought to think of his Presidential vote as the equivalent in money value of one year's salary — saved or thrown away — perhaps he might take the job of selecting the President more seriously. He might be less inclined to heed the words of the character in Gilbert and Sullivan's *Pinafore*, who sang: "I always voted at my party's call and I never thought of thinking for myself at all."

6 White, *op. cit.*, p. 258.

III

ISSUES IN THE PRESIDENTIAL
ELECTIONS, 1968
A DEMOCRATIC VIEW

by

JAMES C. WRIGHT, JR.
Congressman from Fort Worth

CONGRESSMAN JAMES C. WRIGHT, JR., *of the Twelfth District of Texas, spoke on April 19, 1968, at the Second Symposium on Presidential Elections. Thus far in advance of the actual elections, he obviously had little to say about candidates and the campaign. He is convinced "that politics is as absolutely necessary to the functioning of a free society as water is to the flowing of a river." His words are first directed toward some of the big realities of our time — with faster travel and improved communication, the world is now as accessible to each of us as the neighborhood was in former times; science and technology are burgeoning; population has exploded; there has been a revolution of rising expectations, within which men throughout the world are impatient to receive the benefits that the modern world can provide — and then the Congressman gives a ringing and eloquent apology for Lyndon Johnson.*

● THIS YEAR, if you come to participate in a symposium on Presidential politics, you have to have a certain amount of seriousness about you, or at least a pretty good sense of humor.

I am going to assume that you will have some questions, so I should like to ask that each of you, as you think of a question, write it down on a piece of paper. We will have somebody gather them up and bring them here. I will do my best to try to answer them. I am certain there are those to which there simply are no answers. I am equally certain that there are those to which there are valid and factual answers that I do not know. That being the case, I will not try to answer. I will just tell you I do not know, because there is a lot about this business that nobody knows.

Politics and economics vary from the precise exact sciences in that they have a separate ingredient that is never precisely calculated. That is the ingredient of human beings — how they are going to react to certain stimuli, and how they are going to respond to a certain economic movement. This is one of the reasons that these subjects are so human and difficult. And it is also the reason that these are the most supremely challenging subjects in the world.

May I say just briefly, that I congratulate you for being interested in politics — a subject sometimes thought to be sort of dirty. I suppose, gloomily, that there are thousands of voters who catalogue a politician as a fellow as about as sincere as a Victrola or as shallow as a mirror. They think of politics and conjure up a vision of lobbyists with their bags of gold making their annual pilgrimage to the Mecca of their faith. They think of them exercising, behind the scenes through backstage connivance, whatever influence they can bring to bear upon legislators. I suppose there is — or has been — a certain element of truth in such notions. At least in our past some of these things have occurred in various eras of American history.

But let me say to you that politics is as absolutely necessary to the functioning of a free society as water is to the flowing of a river. To pretend to love democracy as an institution and to despise politics is to pretend to honor the product and to despise the process that creates it. Neither the river nor politics has to be dirty, or corrupted, because man has the wisdom, if he has the will, to keep them both clean, to keep them both flowing responsively to the tide. This is the supreme task of the electorate in a democratic society. That may sound a little stilted or stuffy and maybe overly sentimental, but I think it is substantial and I think it is quite true.

I was invited here on the supposition that I am a Democrat — and that is right. I am a Democrat. I am a Democrat without prefix, without suffix and without apology. I am a Democrat because I happen to believe that every citizen, if he is serious about this business of democracy, should involve himself in one or another of the political parties.

Often people make the mistake of feeling pretty grandiloquent, and very clean and wholesome when they say, "I do not involve myself in political parties. I choose the man." Well, that is all right — that is fine. Except that, when you choose the man, you get the party. You get the party he represents, the structure that it comprises. If you just sit back and do not take part in those processes that lead up to the nomination of two men for President and for Vice-President, are you really making a free choice? I think you are not. Look how limited your choice is. Your choice is limited by the activity, the intelligence, and the interest of those people who have engaged themselves actively in the political arena.

If you are serious about being a constructive, responsible, thoughtful, working citizen — as distinguished from a spectator who can sit in the bleachers and let somebody else do it — then I think everybody should involve himself in one or the other of the great political parties of this country.

And to the extent that that political party does not reflect your thinking, I believe that each individual has the opportunity to exercise some influence on that party which is closest to his thinking. Having said that, let me say that I did not come here to make an extremely partisan speech to you, though it may turn out more partisan than I intend.

If we are going to talk about issues, we need to consider realities. Because issues — if they are responsive — grow out of the realities of our time. So very briefly, let us examine the really big realities of this age in which we find ourselves. I am going to name four of them for you. It is not an exhaustive list, but I think these are the most important ones. These are the things with which your Congress and your Administration are grappling in their efforts to shape the future in the way in which you want it.

❈   ❈   ❈   ❈

The first of these big realities of our time is the fantastic compression of time which has shrunk the planet earth and made the world a neighborhood. Today for the purpose of transportation or communications, El Paso is a lot closer to London, Paris, Moscow or Saigon than it was scarcely a generation ago to our own state capital in Austin. You can travel to any of the major cities of the world today more quickly than your father, scarcely more than a generation ago, could travel to Austin. Certainly you can communicate with somebody in any of the major capitals of the world more rapidly than two generations ago you could have communicated with somebody in any of the nearby state capitals.

Put it this way: several years back there was a popular song entitled "How Wide is the Ocean?" How wide is it? In Columbus's day it was 70 days wide. That is how long it took him to cross it. In 1927, Lindberg covered the same distance in 33 hours. In 1961, a B-58 bomber crossed it in 2½ hours. Today the globe-girdling satellites of both the United States and the Soviet Union are covering that identical distance in a little less than 10 minutes. Or put it this way: El Paso by guided missile is about 40 minutes from Moscow.

So the planet has shrunk. We are a neighborhood. Among other things, this means that our decisions in the international realm have got to be right the first time. It has compressed the time of the decision-making process. Where once diplomacy could have been played like a game of chess with all the moves and countermoves painstakingly thought out in advance, this is no longer true. World events move at the pace of a game of table tennis.

For those who are attempting to do the things that make responses come that will be pleasing to the future, it is infinitely more difficult than it once was. This means also that when freedom is threatened in the world, when war threatens or breaks out, a reality has been made of Ernest Hemingway's admonition: ask not for whom the bell tolls — it tolls for thee. I think that is the first of the realities with which we have to cope.

        ❧   ❧   ＊   ❧

The second major reality is that science and technology are speeding ahead at such a blinding rate that they threaten to leave far behind the human arts governing our relationships between ourselves. This is truly serious. There has been more new scientific discovery in the last 25 years than in the 250 years that preceded them. Ninety per cent of the drugs commonly prescribed by our physicians today were not even known at the end of World War II, when I was the age of the students here now. Well, what does this mean? I think among other things that it means that our institutions of governments must keep pace. It means that education at every level is an absolute necessity — no longer just a nice idea.

For we must make a reality of the dream in this land that the humblest youngster, born of the most deprived circumstances, has as his birthright as much education as he can absorb, and as much as his talents and proclivities will let him take — every child, regardless of his background, regardless of his race, regardless of anything else — every child in this land.

This means education in every realm at this time. It means the Head Start Program. It means the Job Corps Program. It means specialized job training. It probably means some techniques and devices that we have not yet invented or discovered. It means that in attempting these devices, we are going to make mistakes. But, in the very making of those mistakes, we are going to be learning some things that we need to know.

Some people are critical of the Job Corps. Some people say that 30 per cent of the trainees drop out before they complete the training. Well, if we accept that figure, let us talk about it. First, let us realize that 100 per cent of these trainees were already dropouts from schools. If you can redeem 70 per cent of 100 dropouts, I believe that you have achieved a significant success — not a failure. We have got continually to improve all the techniques of education, in depth as well as in breadth. We have got to fan out and promote knowledge in the social sciences as well as the exact sciences, so that our younger generation can keep up with the changing events in the world. Walter Lippmann, in his book, *The Public Philosophy*, raises a serious question as to whether a society such as ours, which depends in the ultimate analysis on public support for major public policies, can survive the stresses and strains of a world grown suddenly small and keenly demanding. I say we must, and to that end, education is an imperative public necessity.

The average blue collar industrial worker changes jobs fifteen times in the course of his career because of automation. So rapidly are old processes being made obsolete that he has to be trained and retrained three times. There are fewer and fewer blue collar jobs, fewer and fewer opportunities for unskilled labor in our rapidly advancing automated society. This highlights the importance of education.

* * * *

The third big reality that we have to recognize and try to cope with is the population explosion. The world's population is growing by geometric progression. In the beginning of the Christian era, there were about 250 million people in the whole world. Within our lifetime — perhaps in the next decade — we are going to have about that many right here in the United States, on only about seven per cent of the world's land surface.

It took our progenitors about 3,000 years to develop the population of three billion people that coexist on our earth at this time. We are doubling that in 30 years. In three decades, we are adding to the living total of the world's population as many as it took our ancestors three millennia to put on the face of the earth. What does this mean?

It means that conservation becomes imperative. Every ounce of top soil we save, every drop of water we can conserve and utilize, every drop of rainfall we can hold and store and put where we need it, every stream we can cleanse from pollution, every ore and mineral we can develop to its utmost — these will be among the finest investments we can make for the future generations.

Right here in the United States we are growing so fast that about every month we have a new El Paso, every year we have more than the equivalent of the state of Maryland. We are growing too fast. That means we face the central necessity in this country, because of this blinding rate of growth, to produce two million new jobs in the private economy every year, if we are to avoid increasing unemployment. It takes two million new jobs annually to make up the slack created by automation and to provide for the workers newly coming on the job market every year.

This has got to be done in the private sector of the economy. Government has got to provide the stimulus. It has got to help create the climate. It has got to offer the inducement and the incentive for enterprise to expand, to invest, to create new organisms of employment so that people can have jobs. This is a new political concept. It is not the same concept that we had in the New Deal days. In those days it was sort of a Keynesian philosophy. This is wholly post-Keynesian.

Last February we completed seven years of continuous economic expansion. This is the longest unbroken period of economic growth, unmarred by any ripple of recessionary trend, in the entire history of the United States. During that time, the Gross National Product increased by a little better than 50 per cent; average family income increased 52 per cent; business profits increased 54 per cent. All these things happened in the last seven years.

Yes, prices increased, too. We face the challenge of trying to create a general relative stability of prices within a growing economy, and that is pretty tough. We are not doing quite so well at the task this year. But if you look at the past seven years, the price structure has increased eighteen per cent during the time when the average family income has increased 52 per cent. Any way you look at it, you can buy more things than the average family could buy seven years ago.

I am conscious of the fact that our growth and improvement is not nearly impressive enough, particularly for people in college today. There is a great line in a play called the "Angry Young Men." It is the story of a member of the British Parliament who is fully accepted in all the social and economic circles of Great Britain. His daughter marries a militant young radical, and you can imagine the turmoil this creates in the household.

Ultimately, the father comes to take the girl home and begins berating the idiocy of this boy who stands against everything to which he has devoted his life. Finally the girl breaks into bitter tears and says: "Father, don't you see that you are both angry? You're angry because the world is changing so fast, and he's angry because the world's changing so slowly."

Here I am 45 years old, the father of four kids, and I recognize that for me to talk to my children about the Depression, or about the period between the wars, is almost like trying to talk to them about the Industrial Revolution, which began some 200 years ago. But that is all right. This generation should not be satisfied with the achievements of the past. We have to move ahead still farther and faster, and we have to achieve much more — in a still more compressed period of time.

* * * *

The fourth reality of our time has been called the revolution of rising expectations — and believe me, it is a reality. In every far corner of the earth, from the ancient Middle-Eastern desert to the far-off mountain regions of Tibet, to the smouldering cities of the Orient and the jungles of the underdeveloped countries, men and women are awakening suddenly from a sort of Rip Van Winkle slumber of many generations. They are realizing that people do not have to live the way they have been living for generations. One of the reasons they realize this is because of our improved communication.

People recognize now that it is not necessarily acceptable or necessarily inevitable to live in a society where 60 per cent of the children die before the age of 25, or where 40 per cent of them die before puberty. They recognize that it is not necessarily inevitable that they live in a society where 90 per cent of the land is owned by less than 10 per cent of the people, where the rest of them have really no opportunity to get an education or to borrow enough money to get a piece of land. For they know that other societies have breached that barrier.

These people are expecting improvement — not in some distant generation, but in their time. No longer are they content to sit back and think that we are making some progress toward this. Put yourself in the shoes of the fellow in Cuba under Batista, before Castro came. Eighty-three per cent of the land was owned by twelve per cent of the people. Perhaps 80 per cent of the people did not own one penny's worth of equity in any property, did not own one penny's worth of equity in the hovels they lived in. They were sort of indentured servants, deeply in debt to the landlord. Into this scene strides Castro with his patented panaceas and his promises, pointing with envy to all the big estates — some of them owned by North Americans — and saying, "Follow me and I'll break them up and give them to you!" Well, of course, it was a cruel hoax, utterly impossible of fulfillment. But let us remember the plight of the people to whom he was talking. Put yourself in their spot. Here is a man whose little girl comes to him with eyes that say, "Daddy can move mountains." But he cannot put food in her empty stomach, and he knows that if his child gets sick he cannot get a doctor. He knows that his child will not have a chance to go to college any more than he had a chance to go to college. He knows that unless something different comes, his child is not going to have a chance at all. This is a desperate man, you see, and he is ready to accept any promise that anyone offers him that there might be a better mañana. This is the challenge we face all over the world, in all the underdeveloped countries. The challenge is not just to say to them that communism is wrong. Of course it is wrong. But, the challenge is to demonstrate to them that there is a way — and a better way — by which they can fulfill their legitimate economic and social objectives without sacrificing their political liberties.

There is the challenge. That is why we have a Peace Corps. That is why we have a foreign aid program. That is why we have an Alliance for Progress. Sure, we make mistakes. Sure, we waste some money on those efforts. But we need to be doing much more than we are doing, because time is running out, and the opportunity is not going to be there forever.

Let me say that the revolution of rising expectations applies not only around the world — it applies right here in the United States. It is not good enough simply to point out to the minority groups that we have made some progress, because they are like the boy who was angry because the world was changing so slowly. Let us look at it from their point of view. They see television and they see the advertisement telling you to fly the friendly skies of United and they know they cannot fly any sky. Everything they see in the public media is directed to advertising the great affluence of our society. With all that greatness, we do have the responsibility of reaching out and finding those pockets where it has not spread, and creating the infrastructure that will let it spread to them, so that they can participate in the affluence they see. It is not going to be achieved simply by passing open housing bills. Even though I voted for this bill last week, I do not want anybody to get false promises out of it. Some of my good friends did not vote for it — perhaps they thought it would be a false promise. I voted for it simply because I think it is right. We are not arguing about that. But what I am saying is that this particular bill is not going to solve the problem. It does not do any good to tell a man that he has the legal right to come over and buy a house in the nicest part of town if he does not have the money. The house costs maybe $50,000 and he cannot get that unless he has training and some skills to apply to that job.

Four million Negroes moved from the agricultural South in the last two decades — driven out by the mechanization of agriculture and lured by the better wages in the cities. Deeply disappointed that there were not any jobs for the skills they had, fathers go out searching for other jobs and they do not find any, so they leave a matriarchal society. You see some of the jumbles of row houses — kid with no place to play except in the streets, no open spaces, no one to look up to, and no hope. And they see society all around them wallowing in great affluence.

What the people in ghetto areas need is a rethinking of urban renewal. One of the greatest urban renewal efforts in the world has been in Washington, D.C. The whole southwest quadrant of that city has been transformed since I have been in Congress. From a vermin-invested area of row houses, unfit for human habitation, it was changed into a real Mecca — a beautiful vista of wide, spacious lawns, high-rise apartment buildings, beautiful churches and shopping centers. But the poor people who once lived there were renting the places for $20 to $50 a month, and the places we have built in their stead rent for $300 a month. So what have we done for the ghetto dwellers?

We have got to have rethinking of this, for each family we put out of one of these substandard units, we must guarantee that we put in a good low-cost unit that the family can afford. We must put the emphasis on job training, on practical education, on the ability to get credit at less than usurious rates — on some really practical things. And yet, even with all our society will be able to do, we will not be able to satisfy all the unspoken yearnings, hopes and wants in the cities and ghettos of our country. The best we can do is simply the best we can.

*　*　*　*

I happen to believe that the Democratic Party is the best equipped to do it, but I am not arguing with anybody who says it is not. We have not been perfect. We have been far from perfect. But I think that, in an imperfect society, made up of fallible, mortal creatures, prone to error and prone to mistakes, the Democratic Party really has a pretty impressive record.

Tonight I want to say a few kind words for the President of the United States — both for the awesome office, which has been described as the world's splendid misery, and for the extraordinary and dedicated man who occupies that office. Alexander Hamilton warned of the supreme importance in a democracy to guard not only against the government's oppression of the people, but also against the people's abuse of their leaders. History shows that we have followed that last bit of advice rather badly.

It seems that our strongest and most dedicated Presidents have been those for whom we have reserved our bitterest abuse. George Washington wrote, upon retiring from the office of the Presidency, that he would rather be in his grave than back in the White House suffering the monumental accusations and nasty personal innuendos to which he, George Washington, had been subjected. It is hard to believe, because we think of him as a beatified figure. Thomas Jefferson was called by his detractors a Jacobin and in that day, I suppose, that was equivalent to calling a man a socialist or a communist sympathizer. One of his contemporaries wrote these words: "The Republic is in its last stages because that atheist from Virginia is in the White House." Well, Thomas Jefferson was not an atheist, of course. But all Presidents have been called dirty names. No President has been more bitterly reviled in the press, from the pulpit, on the street corner and in the Congress than Abraham Lincoln, whom we think of today as sort of a sainted figure. The political cartoons of his day were in such bad taste that they would make today's cartoonists blush with shame. One fellow whom Lincoln later honored by appointing him to his cabinet even went so far as to say that a big game hunter was a fool to go all the way to Africa to search for a gorilla, when "the original gorilla sits at this moment in the White House, scratching himself." That is the way they talked about Lincoln. Both Roosevelts also were subjected to this type of vilification.

In 1908, there was a magazine called the *American Businessmen*. It looked somewhat like *Forbes, Harper's* or the *Atlantic Monthly*. On the front cover of the *American Businessman* was a picture of Teddy Roosevelt, with a crown on his head. The caption underneath asked, "Shall he be our King?" The lead editorial contained this sentence: "His policies are leading us down the dead end path toward socialism!" And remember — it is Teddy Roosevelt I am talking about, not Franklin D. I am talking about 1908, not 1938.

All of us remember the ugly, dirty, mean little things that were said about John F. Kennedy — including the attacks on his personal motives and his personal life — though we may try to forget. I think all of us, in the trauma of his assassination were overcome by a temporary shame, and we realized — for a little while — how shabbily we treat our Presidents.

Now, the hounds of the hunt are in full cry again. The quadrennial silly season of overstatement is upon us, and like some weird cult we turn upon our leader and try to devour him.

Let me make it clear that I am not talking about those who criticized American policy constructively and creatively and responsibly, or those who honestly and honorably disagree with the President on matters of opinion. I am talking about those who wallow in the gutter of personal abuse; those who are forever assailing the President's motives; those who trade in fear and traffic in hatred; and those who superciliously set themselves above the President of the United States to sneer at his works, mistrust his words, belittle his deeds and even question his honor.

I am talking about a few urban sophisticates who think they have invented a safe and clever way to criticize the integrity of the President of the United States by inventing a term they call the "credibility gap" and chattering about it incessantly in hopes that they can create a wedge of disbelief between the American people and their elected leaders. I am talking about some who gleefully try to thwart the President in his international commitments — in the making of which he was speaking for all of us under the Constitution — and try to embarrass him internationally.

I had the privilege in 1960 to take to the floor of the House of Representatives a bill President Eisenhower very much wanted to be passed. It was a bill to create in Washington a permanent headquarters site for the Pan American Health Organization, the oldest regional health organization in the world, the oldest part of the Organization of American States. The group had formally voted to accept the invitation to locate its headquarters in Washington, and the bill came out to ratify it. It came through my committee and I was given the responsibility of handling it on the floor. Because it was the last part of the session, the bill had to come on what is called a suspension of the rules, and we had only 40 minutes to debate both sides and then vote it up by a two-thirds majority. Otherwise the bill would not pass.

Mr. Rayburn called me up and said, "Jim, there is an unholy alliance here. Your bill is in trouble, for there are some in my party who are seizing upon this as a means of embarrassing President Eisenhower. There are some in my party who are of the isolation syndrome who hate anything of an international character, and they are going to put together one-third of the votes to defeat Eisenhower." Now I had reserved three minutes to close debate, and I racked my brain for something to say and this is what came to me. I said, "We have only one President at a time, and he's President for all of us. I didn't vote for this President. But he is my President. And if he's embarrassed, I'm embarrassed, because my country is embarrassed."

And this thought came: "If all of us were flying over the ocean in an aircraft together, we might not have picked the pilot. But I'll be darned if any of us would put water in the gasoline tank just to embarrass the pilot." I believed that when Dwight D. Eisenhower was President. I believed that when John F. Kennedy was President. And I believe it now that Lyndon B. Johnson is President.

The most bitter partisan critics of President Johnson should recall that it was he, as Senate majority leader, who fashioned and carried out the responsible and bipartisan policy that permitted President Eisenhower to exercise that responsibility which is invested in him by the Constitution.

Because of Lyndon Johnson's sense of restraint and responsibility to his country, there was no doubt anywhere in the world that however divided we were at home, we faced the world as one, united. Never has a man come better qualified for the presidency by background, knowledge, experience, and infinite familiarity of not only the institutions of government, but also the people that make up those institutions. Never has anybody sacrificed more of his personal repose or worked harder to fulfill his promises to the American people, and no President has kept more of his promises to the American people than has Lyndon Johnson.

For generations, every presidential candidate has been talking about a day when we would have medical care for the aged, so that the twilight years might be golden years of happiness and fulfillment instead of gray years of need and neglect. It remained for Lyndon Johnson and the Eighty-Ninth Congress to make that a reality. For generations every presidential candidate has been saying we want to equalize educational opportunity. Yet it remained for Lyndon Johnson and the Eighty-Ninth Congress to make a reality of equalized educational opportunity. In the last three years, we have appropriated more money in the Congress for educational purposes than was appropriated in all the 170 some odd years prior to that.

For generations, every candidate has been saying that he was going to do something to equalize opportunity and to provide fair treatment of the minority. It remained largely for Lyndon Johnson and his Administration to carry out the actual fulfillment of the civil rights programs. And for these efforts he is rewarded with abuse. The white supremacists rail at him for passing the greatest volume of civil rights legislation in history. The black power militants castigate him for not having done the impossible, immediately. The reactionaries attack him for passing the greatest volume of social legislation in history. The self-styled New Left berates him for defending those very institutions of government and society which he has sworn duty to defend. One group flails at him for spending too much on Vietnam and too little on domestic programs, and the other extreme attacks him for spending too much on domestic programs and too little on Vietnam. They cannot both be right. Each extreme is entirely too eager to criticize and too reluctant to analyze.

Any President — and particularly this President — deserves something better than this. At the very minimum he deserves the assumption of our good faith, our understanding, and our support when we can give it. If we cannot uphold him in the international realm, at least we ought not undermine him.

* * * *

I am glad to have been here today. I hope what I have said bears upon campaign issues. At any rate, this is the field out of which campaign issues are going to grow. We must look not for slogans, but for solutions.

I am a Democrat because I think ours is the better of the two parties. It is most responsive to the needs of the people. It is the party grounded in the soil of all the people. I think it is the best instrument of human will that has been put together as a political entity.

Whether you want to be a Democrat or a Republican, I urge you to do several things: do not look for scapegoats, look for solutions. Do not try to tear this country apart, try to unite it. Do not try to hate people, try to love them and try to create the basis for a reconciliation. If you do these things, I do not care what you call yourself. You can be a democrat with a little "d." That is all that counts.

IV

THE EMPTY HEAD BLUES:
Black Rebellion and White Reaction

by

AARON WILDAVSKY
University of California at Berkeley

April, 1968

PROFESSOR WILDAVSKY's *contribution to the first Presidential Symposium in April, 1967, was a spirited and extremely well received extemporaneous presentation. His contribution to this symposium is not directly related to the mechanics of elections and campaigns; rather it provides a stimulating and challenging analysis of one of the most divisive of the problems that face the nation, one with which all presidents and candidates for the office must deal.*

His conclusions are that nearly all of the palliatives currently being offered are too little, too late, and too remote from realization; that massive remedies must be effectuated, and at local levels yet, popularly attractive or not; and that, whatever course is to be followed, our dilemma is certain to become intensified before acceptable solutions to it appear.

● LIBERALS HAVE BEEN MOANING those empty head blues. They feel bad. They know the sky is about to fall in. But they cannot think of anything to do. Too sanguine and too self-righteous about their part in the civil rights movement, they are too easily prey to despair when their contribution is rejected by those they presumed to help. Torn between a nagging guilt and a secret desire to turn on their black tormentors, white liberals have become spectators watching with frozen horror as their integrationist ideals and favorite public programs disintegrate amidst violent black rebellion. How did this maddening situation come about? What can be done about it?

How to Enrage Whites Without Helping Blacks

A recipe for violence: Promise a lot; deliver a little. Lead people to believe they will be much better off but let there be no dramatic improvement. Try a variety of small programs, each interesting but marginal in impact and severely underfinanced. Avoid any attempted

{ 44 }

solution remotely comparable in size to the dimensions of the problem you are trying to solve. Have middle-class civil servants hire upper-class student radicals to use lower-class Negroes as a battering ram against the existing local political systems. Then complain that people are going around disrupting things and chastise local politicians for not cooperating with those out to do them in. Get some poor people involved in local decision-making, only to discover that there is not enough at stake to be worth bothering about. Feel guilty about what has happened to black people. Tell them you are surprised they have not revolted before. Express shock and dismay when they follow your advice. Go in for a little force, just enough to anger, not enough to discourage. Feel guilty again. Say you are surprised that worse has not happened. Alternate with a little suppression. Mix well, apply a match, and run. . . .

The dilemma of liberal politicians is exquisite. Now they play only "minus-sum" games in which every player leaves the contest worse off than when he entered. The first rule is to get yourself hooked on purely symbolic issues. This guarantees that if you fail to get your policy adopted you are revealed as impotent and useless to the deprived. If you win your policy objective, you are even worse off because it is soon clear that nothing has changed. A typical game played under this rule is called "Civilian Police Review Board." The objective is to force a racist response from the voters who are fearful of their safety on subways and in the streets. The game begins with a publicity campaign focusing on fascist police, various atrocities, and other lurid events. The police and their friends counter with an equally illuminating defense; nothing is wrong that a little get-tough campaign would not cure. The game ends with a ballot in which white voters are asked to choose between their friendly neighborhood policeman and the spectre of black violence. The usual result is that the whites vote for the police and defeat the review board. If a review board is created, however, it soon becomes apparent that a few judgments against policemen have no effect on the critical problem of securing adequate police protection for Negroes. But the game is a perfect loser: everyone's feelings are exacerbated and the conflict continues at a new height of hostility.

There are many similar games. In Milwaukee, for example, wave after wave of Negro demonstrators cry out for a fair housing ordinance. The certain result is that Caucasians are made furious. The sad thing is that if the punitive marches succeed in their immediate goal, only a handful of Negroes at most will be helped. Or consider the drive to achieve school integration by busing children to different parts of the city. If such integration is accompanied by huge efforts to create equality of educational achievement among black and white, all praise is due. But if black children still read poorly, race hatred may well increase. Black radicals will then be certain to condemn the liberal integrationists who have again left them and their children holding an empty bag.

The liberal politician is damned if he does and damned if he doesn't. He breaks his back to get two historic civil rights acts passed only to find himself accused of coming in too little and too late. The rat control bill is a perfect example of the classic bind. When Congress originally failed to pass the bill, it was made into a bitter example of inhumanity. Yet it can safely be said that had the bill sailed through Congress it would also have joined the list of those liberal measures that are not good enough to do the job. Too little and too late. How much all this is like Groucho Marx's famous crack that any country club willing to have him as a member was not exclusive enough for him to join.

We have learned some hard lessons. Every time we try to deal with problems of race we end up with symbolic gestures that infuriate everyone and please no one. Why? The American dilemma is a compound of racism suffused with class differences. Since America appears to be richer in economic resources than in racial respect, it would be natural to tackle economic problems first. Few of us expect a quick solution to the lesser problems posed by large class differences among white people. No one is surprised that upper-class whites do not integrate with their lower-class racial cohorts. Yet we persist in following policies that attack racism before economic equality has begun to be established. The result is that neither poverty nor racism is diminished.

Disheartened by the magnitude of the change required in racial behavior, unwilling to recognize the full extent of the resources required to improve economic conditions, we are tempted to try a lot of small programs that create an illusion of activity, ferment, and change. But nothing much happens. Providing many little economic programs increases demands for more without the means of fulfillment. Confusion is rampant because it looks to some (mostly white) like so much is being done, and to others (mostly black) that nothing is happening. Hence the rival accusations of black ingratitude and white indifference. It is apparent that we should abandon symbolic policies that anger whites and do not help blacks and should concentrate instead on programs that will materially increase the well-being of poor people in the United States. Programs should be large rather than small. They should provide tangible benefits to many citizens, not symbolic rewards for a few.

Income and Education

The most compelling need is for a fast and vast job program designed virtually to end unemployment among Negroes. The best alternative would be a super-heated economy in which jobs searched for people and employers served their own interests by training any available man. Inflation would be a problem but one of much lesser magnitude than present dilemmas. The next best alternative would be large government subsidies to finance decent jobs with futures, again leaving training to employers and motivation to indigenous groups and the near-universal desire for legitimate gain. Nothing else is possible until we end high rates of unemployment.

But any program designed to improve the longer range prospects of the disadvantaged would also have to involve a fundamental change in elementary education. There are many things we do not know about improving education. But we do know that the child who reads well can do most anything and the child who cannot is lost. If you are fourteen and cannot read, you know there is no future for you in ordinary American life. Following the principle of "bottleneck" planning (i.e., concentrating every effort on the most critical resources), one would abolish all subjects in the curriculum except reading and a little mathematics. Every six months there would be examinations in reading, and teachers whose classes fell behind would be held to account. Principals would be promoted on the basis of the accomplishment of their students in reading. Although family conditions may overwhelm all other factors in ability to learn, as the Coleman report suggests, this is a conclusion to which we should be driven only after making the absolute maximum effort to get every child to read.

Would these employment, income, and education policies stop black rebellions?[1] That is bound to be the question. Alas, it is a mean-spirited question because it deflects attention from human needs. But it will raise itself insistently, so we had better attend to it, especially if (as I believe) rebellions are bound to increase for a time. Let us assess the adequacy of these remedies by evaluating them in the context of theories of racial rebellion.

---

[1] One has to be careful not to commit semantic aggression. The word "riot" is too aimless to apply to a phenomenon that is national in scope and is clearly directed at expressing rage against the conditions of life of black people. To use "revolt," however, would suggest far more leadership, organization and concerted action than appears to have been the case. So we are left with "rebellion," an appropriate word to designate violence by people who wish to express their hostility toward prevailing conditions but who are not yet organized to attack the larger society.

Reward and Blackmail Theories

We are everywhere confronted with exceedingly primitive notions of the causes of racial disturbances. According to one popular model, rebellions are caused by giving rewards to the people who engage in these activities. The reward theory posits ever-increasing violence in response to the hope of getting ever-increasing rewards. This vulgarized version of learning theory (Christians call it sinning to abound in grace) suggests that violent outbursts will continue so long as Negroes get rewards in the form of governmental policies designed to improve their conditions. Would it be true, then, that the less that is done for Negroes the less the probability of racial rebellion? What will we do when at all future moments we will be looking back at past rebellions, passing through present rebellions, and anticipating future rebellions?

Another currently-held model suggests that white people help black people only because black people rebel. Blackmail is an appropriate designation for this theory. Rebellions by blacks cause whites to provide rewards; these rewards presumably lead to a reduction in hostility. But, on this theory, a decrease in hostility inevitably leads to a lesser willingness by whites to give rewards to blacks. Hence there will be more riots.

Obviously, if one begins by assuming a connection between riots and rewards, one can only conclude that riots cause rewards or rewards cause riots. Disaster is predicted if help is given and doom if it is not. Perhaps a slightly more complex analysis would be helpful.

The Theory of Relative Deprivation

America is a country to which people who were worse off have come to be better off. And so it has proved to be for most of us. But not for Negroes. Not in slavery and not afterwards. The southern system of slavery so effectively cut off Negroes from former home, family and culture that comparisons with the past that sustained so many others against the initial adversity of life in America became meaningless. Being better off than in slavery hardly recommends itself to anyone as a criterion of judgment. For better or worse, black men have been born anew in America. Negroes can only compare their positions to their recent past or to others in America. They have evidently chosen to be Americans if they can. That is our common hope. But it can also be our despair because it is so difficult to satisfy people whose standard of comparison is the richest segment of the richest nation on earth.

Imagine that our fondest dreams were realized: we had secured virtually full employment and higher income for Negroes as well as other Americans. There would certainly be an improvement in the Negro condition. But there would also be an increase in "relative deprivation." The higher starting point for other Americans would guarantee that result. The arithmetic follows:

Assume that Negroes make $4,000 a year and that other Americans they compare themselves with make $10,000 a year. If whites increased their income 5 per cent a year, Negroes would have to gain an incredible 15 per cent a year in order to gain equality of income in ten years. If we take the more reasonable assumption about the best that could happen — a 10 per cent increase per year for Negroes and a 5 per cent for others — the absolute difference in income would actually continue to increase for the first decade! So, if rebellions are caused in part by relative deprivation — by resentment at inequality — and not merely by absolute deprivation, there will be more rebellions.

Now take education. The most optimistic assumption about education would be that the gap between whites and blacks would narrow significantly in ten or twenty years and not sooner. While the quality of education might improve significantly and quickly if we are very lucky, the benefits would take time to manifest themselves. Moreover, higher educational achievement, while desirable in itself, would likely lead to still higher aspirations. Ergo: things will get worse before they get better.

Job, income, and education policies may be necessary to stop rebellions in the future but they will not suffice to halt them now. Before accepting this melancholy conclusion as the final sentence on our racial crimes, let us see if a closer look at black rebellion will not suggest to us additional remedies.

The Anger Plus Opportunity Theory

The most straightforward explanation of riotous behavior is that the violence is a combination of anger and opportunity. That whites have long despised Negroes is no secret. That Negroes suffer numerous indignities on account of their color is all too evident. When extraordinary levels of unemployment running as high as 30 per cent for black youth, are added to these daily causes of resentment, it is no wonder that many Negroes feel enraged. But it is one thing to feel mad and angry and another to feel safe enough to act out those feelings. The relative lack of black violence in the South may be partly attributed to the well-founded fear by Negroes that severe retribution will be visited upon them. Just as soon as Negro strength increased sufficiently in northern cities and whites became troubled about brutal retaliation, it became safer for Negroes to act on violent feelings. The faint stirrings of white conscience may have had the paradoxical effect of legitimizing black violence without simultaneously leading to actions that dramatically alleviated oppressive conditions. Support for this hypothesis comes from a study of anti-white violence in Africa, which shows that there was little bloodshed in countries that engaged either in consistent repression or gave independence to the black majority; violence did occur when whites vacillated.

To the degree that this overly simple theory is correct, it also helps explain the essential perversity of the racial situation. The theory implies that one way of mitigating violence would be to reduce the pattern of injustice that gives rise to feelings of rage. So far so good. But recognition of the problem, mobilizing poltical support to begin to act, requires widespread and intense dissemination of information on just how bad things were and continue to be. The message to Negroes is that they have been and are being treated badly. There cannot help but be the suggestion that Negroes are justified in taking strong actions to improve their position. There are bound to be white people whose guilt disarms them when faced with destructive acts. Thus the laudatory effort to reduce the desire of Negroes to act violently actually increases their opportunities for using force without the corresponding expectation of severe punishment. The two sides of the desire-plus-opportunities theory of racial violence are not in balance; attempts to reduce the desire have the exasperating effect of increasing the opportunity.

Violence reduced support for measures designed to help Negroes. Yet the polar opposite tactic — non-violent pressure — is impossible to maintain. The emphasis of the civil rights movement on non-violence was unnatural. It reassured whites and helped get bills on voting rights passed in Congress. But it left no place for what used to be called the manly art of self-defense. Where was all that black rage to go? The Black Muslims, who have always stressed self-defense, have not yet joined in violent rebellion. Instead of a normal stress on self-defense, however, many Negro activists have shifted from turning the other cheek to abusing the man. One extreme has simply been substituted for another.

In such a situation it is easy for black men to succumb to a politics of outrage in which violent rhetoric provides a substitute for action that results in helping their brothers. Caught between rage and impotence, held responsible by no mass following of their own, Negro spokesmen compete in ragging the white man. Negroes cannot help enjoying the fun, but we should be as clear as they are that the whole act is directed toward "Whitey." If who a man loves can be determined by who he cannot resist talking to, then Whitey has captured all the affection these people have. No doubt this perverse form of Uncle Tomism will eventually be exposed by Negroes who want leaders to pay attention to them. In the meantime, we risk the consequences of a rhetoric of violence that angers whites without aiding blacks.

I conclude that all of us in America will need an acute sense of humor to survive the next decade. There will be rebellion if we do the best we know how. There will be even more violence if we do not. Almost harder to bear will be the incredible provocations — mixtures of arrogance, slander, paranoia and duplicity. There are spectacular fantasies among black people about the deaths of Kennedy and Malcolm X right next to saccharine remarks about law and order from whites who have long practiced violence against Negroes. The one truth to which white liberals must now signify is that they do not know, have never known, and will never know anything about black people. Yet one would suppose that if two groups have contact each would have an equal chance of failing to know the other. The old truth may have been that blacks were invisible men for whites. The new truth is that whites are invisible because they all look alike.

The language of "black power" should not, however, be dismissed without serious consideration. The fact that it means so many different things to different men does not prevent our observing that the slogan strikes a responsive chord among black men. At a minimum, black power signifies a widespread concern for a political dimension that has been conspicuously missing from previous theories of racial conflict.

The Identity and Legitimacy Theory

It will add to our understanding if we decide which features of the black rebellions we want to explain. The extensive looting, for example, does not appear especially deserving of explanation. There is looting all over the world when riots occur. That is why martial law is so often declared in the wake of natural disasters. When the police appear uncertain or absent, the urge to loot is apparently more than most of us can resist. Nor do we need to spend an excessive amount of time on the snipers. Virtually every society has small groups with an urge to disrupt its activities. The interesting question is why the mass of citizens did not react against the snipers and the incendiaries who put the torch to their neighborhoods.

The beginning of wisdom about black rebellion is that we are dealing with a problem in social control, with feelings widespread in an entire community, and not with just a few wild men. An entire community has become disaffected. That is not to say Negroes share common views on public policy. Indeed, they can hardly agree on anything. But they will not turn in one of their own to the white man. They will not defend what they have against their own people, not necessarily because they have nothing to lose but because they do not have enough of the one thing that they would otherwise most risk losing——participation in a common American life.

The great question raised by black rebellion is: Who will call himself an American? That has been the modal drama of life in America. Loyalist and patriot, patrician and plebeian, slave and freeman, southern man and northern man, employer and worker, ethnic and wasp, have shattered the quiet of our vast continent with their wars. Today's rebellion is part of this struggle to forge a worthy American identity for black men. Black rebellion presents a crisis of legitimacy – a questioning of "white" authority. Hence the incessant demands for new power relationships. The immediate problems posed by black rebellion are, therefore, political, and require a political response.

Political Solutions

The most obvious political need is for mechanisms to reduce the blatant conflicts between Negroes and police as the most visible and oppressive manifestation of governmental authorities. Increasing the number of Negro policemen (and firemen) would help by blurring the purely racial nature of the encounters. The measures necessary to accomplish this end—allowing entry to people with minor police records, changing various requirements for health and examinations – are within our grasp. Although these policemen may be called black men with white masks, they are still, on the face of it, men of color.

There are also various proposals for altering the role of policemen by putting them more in the role of helpers and by sensitizing them to the problems of life among the severely deprived. It is difficult to quarrel with such humane measures. Yet they do not quite go to the heart of the matter. For policemen do have certain evident law-enforcement functions that may be blurred but not hidden. The rest of us manage to get along with police not through mutual good will but by avoiding contact with them unless we make a specific request for help. Not love but distance is the answer. A substantial increase in employment and rise in income will reduce the opportunity and need for crime. Greater verbal abilities will enable people presently deprived to make rational calculations that they will be better off not breaking the law. Even the dope addict with a higher income is likely to be able to make arrangements that will keep him clear of the police. Relationships with police could be markedly improved by following Jacobus ten Broek's proposal to abolish the law of the poor. One reason that we have "two nations" in America is that there is literally a separate law for poor people. The difficulty is not merely that poor people receive less justice but also that laws about sexual conduct, home finance, drug addiction and dozens of other matters apply to them but not to other Americans. Hiring more Negro policemen will not be successful unless the frequency of unhappy contacts between them and the citizenry is sharply reduced.

Separating men with sticks and guns from the daily lives of citizens may allow us all to breathe a little easier. Even so great an accomplishment, however, does not meet the profound Negro demand for autonomy, for control of some portion of their lives, for the self-esteem that comes from being powerful. If we cast aside the cynicism that tells us no man is truly master of his fate, we can recognize insistent political demands that may be accommodated or crushed but cannot be ignored. For present purposes we can dispense with a lot of research and simply assume that the best way to feel in control is to exercise control. Can this be done at all? Can it be done without generating the violence that will bring about the retribution that ends our hopes?

The usual American response to difficult political problems has been to disperse and fragment them into smaller conflicts that take place in different localities and times. Problems of church and state and education have been handled in just this way. Applying this procedure to racial problems in the past, however, has meant victory for racism or at least the status quo. Deprived of opportunities to exert influence at state and local levels because of official racism or lack of effective political resources, Negroes had no alternative except to look to the national government. This choice of a favored site for conflict was always opportunistic. Calhoun's doctrine of the concurrent majority meant control for regional racists. States rights and local autonomy were doctrines for keeping the Negro and the poor in their places. Now the old men who say that if you live long enough everything comes full circle are justified. Black nationalists, having little hope of a large voice in national and state politics, are talking about local autonomy. They demand a voice and a veto over policies affecting neighborhoods in which black people are in the majority. Bringing government closer to the people is a slogan that is no longer the exclusive property of conservatives. The pursuit of group interest by radical blacks thus creates opportunities for unusual political coalitions.

The Heller proposals for block grants to states, much of which would be distributed to cities, provide a strong basis for agreement. Local government would be strengthened. Negroes would find it more worthwhile to make demands on city governments. Cities would have the resources to grant some of these demands. The formation of neighborhood corporations or governments would be the next step. Run by elected councils within specified geographical boundaries, the corporations would provide a forum for airing grievances and working out common demands. In order to avoid complete focus on demands and to provide experience in self-government, the neighborhood corporations would also negotiate with the city government to take over certain limited functions. Education has long been considered a neighborhood function and there are already moves toward further decentralization. If health and housing inspections are serious sources of grievances, cities may be willing to let neighborhood corporations hire and guide local people to do the job. Part of the energies within the neighborhood would thus be devoted to resolving disagreements among the local people about how they should run their own affairs.

We should be clear about what we are doing. The neighborhood corporation involves a return to earlier patterns of local rule that were regarded as offensive to principles of good government. The movement from the spoils system to neutral competence through civil service will, for a time, be reversed. What were previously despised as the worst attributes of boss rule and ethnic depravity — favoritism, trading of jobs for favors, winking at abuses when perpetrated by one's own kind, tolerance of local mores regarded by some as corrupt — will be reinstituted. Political practices worked out to accommodate the needs of lower-class immigrants, arrangements abandoned when they conflicted with rising professionalism and economic status, may understandably be preferred by underprivileged black people. The uneven development of all our people makes it difficult to pursue national practices. Negroes mirror the problem. They will have to reconcile the fact that programs that permit greater autonomy for urban Negroes may leave rural Negroes at the mercy of hostile state and local governments.

Today the black ghettoes resemble nothing so much as newly emerging nations faced with extraordinary demands and few resources. There is the same ambivalence toward "foreign" aid: you must have it and yet you hate the giver because of your dependence on him. Highly educated and skilled people (black as well as white) are deeply resented because of the well-founded fear that they will take things over, a process analogous to the "Red-expert" feuds that have plagued Russia and China. The greater the disparity between aims and accomplishments, the greater the demagoguery and destructive fantasy life. Yet underneath the pounding rhetoric there are men and women who are learning the skills of leadership. They must be given a chance to learn, that is, to make mistakes. They must have an opportunity to generate growth in human resources in their own communities. Otherwise, they will lack the pride and security to re-enter American life on conditions of mutual interest, respect and allegiance.

We need to be reminded, however, that without a drastic decrease in unemployment no other programs will be meaningful. It will prove extraordinary difficult to abolish the law of the poor because so many people will be dependent on governmental assistance that the tax burden will generate additional demands for obnoxious restrictions. When so many men cannot make a living now, educational improvement will seem hopelessly long range. Community action programs suffer the most because of the utter futility of finding local measures to create vast employment. Expectations are raised that no local or state political system can meet. Ordinary politics are discredited. Each generation of community leaders is rejected as soon as it becomes part of "The Establishment" that cannot deliver. The few poor people who do participate drop their activities in disgust because they are unable to control anything worthwhile in comparison to the magnitude of the problems.

Income, education, and power are mutually supportive. Better education will enable Negroes to receive higher income and to gain the communications skills necessary to carry on political activity. The exercise of governmental power will strengthen the sense of mastery that makes the long road of education seem worthwhile. Political power also creates jobs. Good jobs at decent pay provide additional resources for education and political activity. Men who are noted for their strong sense of efficacy, excellent education and good income are the bastions of legitimacy in our political system.

Political Support

What about the political feasibility of the economic and political programs advocated here? Will the President and Congress agree to spend the $5 or $10 billion a year that a job program will cost? Will mayors and city councils agree to share limited powers with neighborhood corporations? Will a policy of suppression appear more attractive as well as less expensive? There is an old story that goes, "Harry, how's your wife?" "Compared to what?" he replies. The political desirability of these programs depends in part on how they compare with what we have been doing. Let us begin with the sad plight of our mayors.

Mayors in the United States are in an incredible position. The only things they can do, such as providing better recreation facilities, improving housing inspection and the like, are strictly marginal improvements. They lack the money and the power to do more. Yet they are held responsible for every evil. Rebellions appear to occur at random, afflicting cities whose mayors try hard to do the right thing and cities whose mayors are indifferent or hostile. What incentives will mayors have to do what good they can do? Since they cannot possibly do enough, the do-nothing mayor appears no worse off than the better mayors. A major possibility is that mayors will learn to concentrate on the one area in which they might do well and reap credit from some segments of the population — suppression of rebellions. Working with neighborhood corporations, linked with receiving fresh infusions of federal funds, should prove attractive to mayors who despair of their present situation.

Politicians in the Democratic Party are frantically pursuing ways of handling racial problems that will not end in disaster for everyone concerned. Buffeted between the hostility of blue-collar workers to civil rights legislation and the inability to satisfy radical Negroes no matter what, the politicians fear their party will be split on racial grounds. They foresee waves of repression and a permanent estrangement between black and white in America.

Consider what a new orientation would have to offer to Democratic Party politicians. They would try to accept inevitable losses graciously. They would not even try to bid for the support of racial radicals, white or black. The Democrats would turn down both mass suppression and mass violence, avoiding especially symbolic issues that embitter whites and do not help blacks. The politicians would espouse primarily policies promising immediate and substantial improvement of the economic condition of poor people. Decent jobs at good pay come first. Next, there should be the most powerful education program that can be devised to enable the presently disadvantaged to participate as equals in the market place and the political arena. These policies should be presented at face value as measures for making good the promise of American life. These policies are consonant with the traditions of the Democratic Party and they need not divide the races. The poor need help. We are a rich nation. We can and should give that help.

No doubt a party promoting these income policies might lose an election or two. But when it did get into power it would have goals worth achieving. The difficulty with existing policies is that even when properly pursued they do not help enough people immediately in direct ways. The usual mode of alleviating difficult problems by incremental attack along diverse fronts does not work because there is no solid base upon which to rest these efforts. We will never know what long-run contributions anti-poverty programs can make if we continue to insist that secondary programs substitute for primary ones, that supporting programs be adopted in place of the basic efforts they are intended to assist.

Democratic divisions provide extraordinary opportunities for Republicans to recover from decades of declining support. The danger is that an anti-Negro stance will appear to offer hope of detaching white voters from the Democratic Party. The resistance of these voters to conservative economic policies would be submerged under a tide of racial anger. There is another stance, however, that would be productive at the polls and fit comfortably with Republican principles. A massive employment program could be expected to win over some Negroes and poor whites while not alienating existing Republican support. Such a program would hold out greater long-run hope of alleviating rebellious conditions than would suppression. Republicans would probably not support Federal subsidies for radical community action. But a program that stressed local autonomy through neighborhood governments should prove attractive to conservatives. Indeed, Republicans are much less weighed down than are Democrats with commitments to existing welfare and education policies that Negroes find so disagreeable.

A Response to Rebellion

There will be rebellions; that much we can take for granted. The question is not whether these things will happen but how Americans will choose to react. It is easy to win tactical victories — disperse mobs brutally — and lose strategic battles. In the midst of consummate gall and endless effrontery, there is considerable danger of committing strategic suicide. What we do should depend on what we want. The prevailing confusion makes it advisable to take the risk of restating the obvious.

Just as Lincoln put preservation of the Union above all else in his times, so should we put construction of a multi-racial nation as our major objective. Our goal is that we all consider ourselves Americans who pay allegiance to the same political symbols and participate as citizens in the same national life. In pursuit of this goal we must reaffirm our dedication to integration of the races for all who wish it. Wholly white or black communities are one mode of participation in a common life. Integration is the preferred way of life for those who believe that there must be a single nation in America. A surface integration, however, must not be pursued at the expense of equality of achievement among black and white, for then integration will become a barrier to creation of a joint American identity.

If we do not wish white and black men to live as citizens in the same country, we will have no difficulty in finding policies appropriate to that end. We can continue what we are doing. Better still, we can let violence feed on violence. The early riots have largely been aimless affairs in which destruction has been visited by Negroes on their own neighborhoods. Mass repressions visited indiscriminately upon black people can give them new reasons for race hatred and further violence. White people can be turned into proto-blacks — people who fear destruction because of their color. The difference between the races is that whites possess more abundant means of committing mayhem.

Americans who wish to hold open the possibility of emerging as a single people should not engage in mass repression. The surest way for black bigots to get a following is for white racists to create it. We want to open and not to foreclose the possibilities of being American together. Yet capitulation to lawless behavior would also be bad. The hunger for humiliation shown by the New Left can only succeed in demeaning everyone. The black man's dignity cannot be won by the white man's degradation. The bread of humiliation will feed few people. The most destructive elements will be encouraged to raise the level of abuse. White anger will rise. Acting out the ritual frenzy of hatred will close all doors.

Yet there will be riots. Our position is that in America one must not be violent. So violent rebellions must be put down. Our aim should be to separate the actively violent from the rest of the black community. Force should be limited, specific, and controlled. A police sniper may be sent after a civilian sniper rather than spraying whole blocks with bullets. Snipers may be left alone while police concentrate upon protecting the lives and property of residents.

Our program is neither suppression nor capitulation but affirmation of common possibilities in a civil society. Without promising what no man can deliver — an end to the rebellions that are the consequences of our past failures — we can try to do what we now see to be right and just. A massive employment program, a concerted effort to improve educational achievement, and then support for a process of self-generating growth in the urban ghettoes.

V

CAMPAIGN PROPAGANDA
IN PERSPECTIVE

by

STANLEY KELLEY, JR.
Princeton University

April, 1968

THE ASSUMPTION *that all the presidential candidate needs is a viable public image — that if he makes it there, he has it made — is gross over-simplification of the complex business of campaigning for the presidency. To be sure, the public campaign is quintessential; but there are also many other campaigns — a whole set of them. There are the campaigns to win the support of the press, to gain financial backing, to enlist interest groups, and to win over dissident party factions. Campaigns are not Roman holidays; "they are an integral part" of the business of governing.*

● THE DAY AFTER ROBERT F. KENNEDY announced his campaign for the presidency, he retained the services of one Charles Guggenheim. Mr. Guggenheim is a man known to very few by name but to a great many by his works: He is among the ablest of those who specialize in the production of television spot announcements for political campaigns. The Kennedy organization's obvious eagerness to sign him up, once the decision had been taken to challenge President Johnson, aptly illustrates the importance that modern campaigners attach to the skills of the professional propagandist.

Today, one-third or more of all the money spent in presidential, gubernatorial, or senatorial campaigns goes more or less directly to pay for propaganda materials or the distribution of propaganda materials. Professional campaign management and consulting firms are now an established feature of our political life, and names like Spencer-Roberts, or Joseph Napolitan, or Whitaker and Baxter, are becoming increasingly familiar to those who read political news with any care. Indeed, one way a modern candidate may indicate his intention to run a serious campaign is by retaining one or another of the better known campaign management firms.

Because some aspects of modern campaign propaganda are both novel and very public, however, the temptation is great for writers on politics to stress them unduly. While one cannot weigh very exactly the importance of propaganda activities as compared to other aspects of campaigning, one can put the role of propaganda in campaigns into a more realistic perspective than it often is. And that is what I hope to do in this paper.

I propose to do so by elaborating upon an idea that I advanced in a very sketchy form in my book, *Political Campaigning:* That all campaigns can fruitfully be viewed as a *set* of campaigns — or sub-campaigns, if you like that term better.

A political campaign is, first of all, a campaign to win the support of the press. Secondly, it is a fund raising campaign. It is, thirdly, a campaign to win or maintain the support of leaders of interest groups and of the interest groups themselves. Fourthly, it is a campaign to win or keep the support of local and state party leaders and their followers in the wards and precincts. And finally, it is a campaign to win the favor and the votes of the great mass of voters. This last aspect of campaigning could be called the "public" campaign — it is the one that comes to us by means of radio and television and newspapers and sound trucks and bumper stickers and buttons. All these "campaigns" go on more or less simultaneously, although campaigning for the support of the mass public is usually concentrated in the last two or three weeks before election day, while the campaign to win the support of interest groups and party activists may be largely over by that time. Each of the campaigns is directed to a different constituency and each involves different techniques.

Let me begin by discussing what I have called the public campaign, since by doing so it is easier to understand why it must necessarily be only a part of the total campaign effort.

The presidential candidates in 1968 will face a potential electorate of something like 118,000,000 people. Of these, somewhere between 70 and 75 million may be expected to vote. What can a candidate do to get enough of these voters to cast their votes for him? A candidate of course is not alone. He has around him an organization made up of his party's national committee, his personal organization, and perhaps the leftovers of the organization that won him his nomination. But this fact only changes the nature of the question a bit. What can a candidate, and the very few people associated with him, do to reach a large enough segment of the electorate so that the election will come out as they want it to come out?

A candidate, facing a campaign, can think of himself as a bundle of *attributes.*

He has, or he has not, a record in public life. If he has a record, he has declared himself on some issues and not on others. He has run an administration that is pockmarked with scandals or one that was not. He has voted for aid to public schools, or for a test ban treaty, or for the Tonkin Gulf resolution, or for ceilings on federal expenditures — or he has not.

The candidate also has certain personal qualities. He is handsome, like John F. Kennedy, or not particularly handsome, like Calvin Coolidge. He has a beautifully timbred voice like Franklin D. Roosevelt, or, perhaps a voice that sounds like a pipe organ that smokes too much, like Everett Dirksen. He may have four beautiful daughters, like Earl Warren. He may have checked groceries like Richard Nixon, played football like Eugene McCarthy, or been a peddler's grandson like Barry Goldwater.

The candidate has certain group affiliations. He is Catholic or Mormon or Quaker; he is Irish-American, or German-American or old-stock American; he is a Democrat or a Republican.

The candidate is not only such a bundle of attributes; he is also someone who, in the course of the campaign, can take certain *actions* with respect to things people will think important.

He can take, or avoid taking, stands on issues — on aid to education or riots or Vietnam. He can identify himself with groups, as John F. Kennedy did on one occasion, when he told an Italo-American audience that Italian blood ran in his veins. He can identify himself with heroes past or present, as in 1960 Nixon identified himself with Dwight D. Eisenhower and John F. Kennedy with Franklin D. Roosevelt.

The possibility of taking such actions, and the attributes that attach to the candidate himself, give the candidate and his friends something to conjure with. I use the term, "conjure," deliberately. The attributes that count for a candidate are the attributes that he *appears to have,* and the actions that count are those that people believe him to have taken. The candidate and his organization cannot control these appearances and beliefs, by any means, but they can try to shape them. They can emphasize the attributes that they think will count in their favor, hide those that they think will not, correct voice deficiencies, change hair cuts, emphasize some issues and not others. They may invent attributes that do not exist. They can, in short, take actions and attributes and translate them into words and pictures and gestures that the world outside can see if it watches and hear if it listens.

And that is just about all they can do, unaided. The candidate's words and pictures and gestures will be unheard and unseen, except by infinitesimally small part of the electorate, unless he can find amplifiers and projection equipment. What he and his organization can do is almost nothing, without media to carry his words to the voters.

Now, some of this task of *mediation* will be virtually costless from the candidate's point of view. The press — newspapers and magazines — will give a running account of his speeches, feature him in pictures, and present personality sketches of him. Television and radio will carry his voice and pictures in newscasts, present him in forums, documentaries, and interviews. But this kind of free mediation has, from the candidate's viewpoint, an important shortcoming: He does not have final say as to which of his words will be reported and in what form they will be reported. He cannot be sure that the propaganda themes he wants to get across will be the ones that will get across, or that what he wants to emphasize about himself will in fact be emphasized by the press.

This gives rise to what I have termed the campaign for the support of the press. Candidates go to quite elaborate lengths to win the sympathy of working reporters, and some are much more successful in this effort than others. In 1960 John F. Kennedy won sympathy from reporters simply by talking to them, off the record, about his plans and strategies. Reporters like to feel they are on the "inside," as most of us do, and Kennedy tried to give them that feeling. Apparently, Richard Nixon did not do nearly so well on this score and, partly for that reason, was not so well treated by the press. The campaign for the support of the press may also involve efforts to woo editors and publishers. Such efforts may not lead to news blatantly slanted in the candidate's favor, although sometimes it does, but simply to subtly more favorable treatment. In some states, in some state campaigns, campaign managers place some advertising not primarily to help their cause with voters, but to win the good will of publishers.

A second way in which candidates may overcome the shortcomings of free mediation is to pay for it. They can go on tour, buy advertising space and time, and present their own radio and television programs. It is in managing such efforts that professional propagandists have the most to offer the lay politician.

Paid mediation, however, is very expensive, and that fact makes it virtually certain that fund-raising will be an essential concern of the modern campaigner.

How much money a candidate can raise is of obvious importance for the kind of campaign he can mount. *When* he is able to raise it will be important, also: One can plan campaign activities efficiently only if one can count on having the right amounts of money at the right times. *Whom* the money comes from is important. Big contributors can be expected to want access to political leaders, at least, and some undoubtedly want more than that. The techniques of fund-raising available, the flow of funds, and likely targets of successful fund-raising appeals, will set limits on what one can do in a campaign, both technically and substantively.

It is conceivable that a candidate and his organization might rely solely on a "public" campaign — fed with funds from a money-raising campaign and buttressed by a campaign for the support of the press — to bring him the votes he needs to win. It is unlikely, however, because a public campaign — even a well-financed one — is subject to some severe limitations.

The candidate knows that many voters will pay little attention to anything said in, or about, campaigns. Their attention will be sporadic, restless, inexact. He knows that many of those who do pay attention will be those least subject to influence — they will watch and listen because they are interested partisans. A candidate knows that the motivation to register and to vote of many people who favor him will be very weak. He knows, or suspects, some voters will be more responsive to personal appeals from those they know, trust, respect, or owe something to, than they will be to his own obviously self-interested appeals for votes. Because all of these things are true, he will try to supplement his public campaign with campaigns to win the support of interest groups and their leaders and of party organizations and their leaders.

It is a great deal easier to find accounts of the public part of a campaign than it is to find accounts of what candidates do to win the support of interest groups. I can illustrate what is involved — or can be involved — however, by considering the activities of President Truman in 1948.

In that year the main objective of organized labor was the repeal of the Taft-Hartley Act, which had just been passed the year before. Union leaders objected to a number of the Act's provisions — in particular, to its restrictions on spending by unions in political campaigns, to the anti-Communist affidavit it required of union leaders, and to the right to enjoin strikes that it extended to the government. At the same time, President Truman was looking for, and badly needed, support. He sought it from organized labor.

It is easy to forget now that organized labor was not, in 1948, a sure source of enthusiastic support for Truman. It is true that he had vetoed the Taft-Hartley Act, but as a Senator he had been a very uncertain friend of unions, and, as President, he had asked that striking miners be drafted into the armed services. Moreover, once the Congress had passed the Taft-Hartley Act over his veto, he had used that feature of the Act that the unions found most objectionable — injunctions against strikes — seven times. Still, labor and President Truman had much to offer each other. The unions were unlikely to find any stronger ally in their efforts to repeal Taft-Hartley, if the President could be induced to adopt that objective as his own. On his side, President Truman could hope for financial support from the unions and their help in getting sympathetic voters to the polls. Truman and union leaders did reach an agreement. Labor worked hard for the re-election of Harry Truman, Truman committed himself publicly and very strongly to repeal the Taft-Hartley Act, and the rest is history.

I think that similar sorts of maneuvers are a frequent incident of political campaigning. I think, that is, that a great deal of bargaining, tacit or open, goes on between candidates and the leaders of interest groups, and that such bargaining is a very important part of the electoral process. If that is true, it is worth noting that this aspect of campaigning is likely to involve techniques very different from those involved in the public campaign. It is possible to believe that image-building appeals are effective in winning the support of the average voter. It is not easy to believe that they greatly influence Walter Reuther, directly at least.

What I have called the campaign for support of party activists can be viewed, like campaign for support of interest groups, as a kind of bargaining process. Candidates, if elected, are in a position to influence the flow of jobs and favors and contracts to members of local organizations or to people whose favor local organizations seek. And local political organizations, if they are going organizations, can put their precinct workers to work for the candidates they favor.

Let me give two illustrations of the way candidates have gone about wooing party activists, the first from the 1952 presidential campaign.

Soon after the nomination of Eisenhower, a strategy group in the Republican National Committee drew up a campaign blueprint. A paragraph from that document is worth quoting:

> Our job can be stated simply. It is to win enough votes to elect the next President of the United States, together with enough Senators and Congressmen to afford working Republican majorities in both branches of Congress.

We must start with the people who are now Republican — the 20 million voters who have stuck with the Republican Party through thick and thin. *They must not be alienated!*

The blueprint went on to say that several million Republicans, particularly the Midwest followers of Senator Taft, could not be counted upon as willing workers or sure votes.

The Eisenhower organization took several steps to meet the situation. The General, first of all, pledged his support to all Republican candidates regardless of their factional allegiance. He appointed Taftites to prominent posts in his campaign organization. He sent Richard Nixon on tour through Ohio, Illinois, and Indiana, to reassure party leaders in those states, and soon toured the Midwest himself. Finally, he had the famous meeting in Morningside Heights with Senator Taft, from which the Senator emerged with a statement. Not the least important part of that statement was the following sentence: "General Eisenhower stated without qualification that in the making of appointments at high levels or low levels there will be no discrimination against anyone because he or she supported me."

In 1964 Senator Goldwater ran a less successful campaign to win the support of party regulars. After winning nomination, the Senator found himself in trouble with many of his party leaders, General Eisenhower among them. In one attempt to remedy the situation, a letter went out from Goldwater's headquarters to each Republican state chairman, asking his advice on the campaign and giving assurances that only persons approved by him would be appointed leaders of Citizens for Goldwater organizations. In another effort toward the same end, the Senator modified his famous statement that "extremism in the defense of liberty is no vice, moderation in the pursuit of justice is no virtue." What he really meant to say, said Goldwater, was that "whole-hearted devotion to liberty is unassailable and half-hearted devotion to justice is indefensible." The new statement, certainly less ringing than the old, was presumably more appealing to the ears of the moderate Republicans nonetheless. Goldwater's last major effort to mollify moderates of his party came in a conference at Hershey, Pennsylvania, during which he declared himself forthrightly in favor of the Eisenhower-Dulles foreign policy, support of the United Nations and the North Atlantic Treaty Organization, and strengthening of the Social Security program. He repudiated the support of "extremists." All of this represented very substantial changes in the tone, if not the substance, of the Senator's campaign. That none of it really achieved its objective must be attributed, I think, to the operation of what might be called the "rats-desert-a-sinking-ship-at-an-accelerating-rate" principle, for the desire of other Republican leaders to iron out their differences with Goldwater seemed to become increasingly small as the Senator's chances for election became increasingly remote. While one cannot say finally how justifiable is the special concern for the views of party activists that candidates show, the probable correct answer is that such concern is quite justified. It is clear that canvassing and registration drives can have a marked impact on the turnout of voters. It is not clear how many local party groups are able to mount effective registration and canvass-ing operations, but some certainly are, and others are thought to be. These facts are enough to make most prudent candidates feel that local party leaders are men with whom they must deal.

Let me bring this exposition of what is involved in political cam-paigns to a close. I have been arguing that the political campaigner's success in winning the favor of the mass public implies simultaneous success in winning support from much more limited constituencies. If this is a correct view, it seems to me that several things follow.

First, it follows that the skills of the professional propagandist, while important, and more important than they used to be, perhaps, are not all-important in campaigns. As I noted at the beginning of my remarks, that simple fact may be overlooked because what the propagandist does in campaigns is so obvious and because the relations of candidates to the press, to interest groups, to party leaders, and to contributors are so difficult to expose.

It follows from what I have been saying, secondly, that one must look beyond the public campaign if one is to understand how the electoral process limits the freedom of men in office to act on issues of public policy without fear of adverse consequences at the polls. The major studies of voting have found that many voters have little or no information about issues and little or no knowledge of how candidates stand on issues. From this fact some have concluded that elected officials have a broad range of discretion with respect to matters of policy. The conclusion seems dubious. It might be warranted if the outcomes of elections were decided only by a candidate's success in wooing voters generally, but they are not. In the more restricted constituencies to which the candidate must also appeal, the positions he takes on issues, publicly or privately, can be expected to count a great deal.

Finally, the view of campaigning I have been outlining helps to make clearer the relation of the electoral process to government. Cam-paigns are frequently discussed, both by political scientists and newspapermen, as if they were only a silly interlude in the otherwise serious business of governing. To treat them in this way is to miss the point badly. The influence of members of elite groups on officeholders — seen by some to be what really counts in the day-to-day activities of government — operates *through* the electoral process, not despite it. Men who govern must be concerned with the popularity of their actions — among members of political elites and among voters generally. Because they are so concerned, a significant part of what they do is either in remembrance of things past — of what they promised to do — or an effort to set the stage for the next campaign and to give advance publicity to its heroes and its villains. Campaigns are thus not a "time-out" in the business of governing — they are an integral part of it.

VI

THE STRATEGIC OUTLOOK FOR THE NATIONAL ELECTIONS OF 1968

by

MILTON C. CUMMINGS, JR.

The Johns Hopkins University

September, 1968

AT THE OUTSET *Professor Cummings suggests "four factors which have a powerful bearing on the overall strategic outlook in most presidential elections: . . . (1) the rating given by the public to the administration in power; (2) the distribution of party identification in the United States — how many Democrats and how many Republicans there are; (3) the nature and content of the issue considerations that seem to be salient in the voters' minds; and (4) . . . the extent to which people like or dislike the presidential nominees."*

After extensive treatment of the decline of the Johnson administration in popular esteem, an exploration of the current situation with the normal democratic majority, a comparison of the attractiveness of the candidates, and an analysis of difficulties in store if no candidate received a majority of the electoral vote, the author sums up the prospects with admirable succinctness: "The issues of the day and the public's appraisal of the incumbent Democratic administration seem to be working to Nixon's advantage. In terms of the popular appeal of the individual candidates, it is probably close to a standoff, and in some ways the candidate who is best able to get his own supporters excited about him is not Nixon, and is not Humphrey, but is George Wallace. Party identification, by contrast, is a factor working to Humphrey's advantage. . . . We could yet become involved in a surprisingly close race."

● THE DISCUSSION of a specific election before the votes are counted always has its dangers, but this year any advance discussion of the politics of 1968 seems to be a particularly hazardous occupation. Consider for a moment what the political scenario appeared likely to be to most observers looking toward the future in January of this year. This was to be the year, you will remember, that Senator Eugene

McCarthy was not supposed to pose a serious threat to President Johnson in New Hampshire, but he did. This was the year that Johnson was generally deemed certain to run for re-election, but he did not. This was the year in which Robert Kennedy announced that he was not going to run for the Presidency, but he did. This was the year in which Michigan's Governor George Romney was going to be Richard Nixon's main opponent in the Republican primaries, and he was not. This was the year Nelson Rockefeller was expected to announce for the presidency in March, and Spiro Agnew, the Governor of Maryland, was going to be one of Governor Rockefeller's strongest supporters. But it did not quite turn out that way. And this was the year when many observers believed that the George Wallace third-party candidacy would, like so many other third-party candidacies in our history, look strong in the spring but very weak in the fall. Yet from late winter until now Governor Wallace's showing in the polls has increased from about 10 per cent to close to 20 per cent of the American electorate. These indicators of Wallace strength could well go down markedly in the remaining five weeks of the campaign, but if the polls are anywhere near the mark, as of now, in late September, there are something like 15 million Americans who are considering voting for George Wallace.

The turbulent events of the last nine months thus stand as a sober warning to anyone who would try to impose order on the scattered elements of the current campaign. Nevertheless, perhaps the strategic situation faced by the parties in 1968 will come into sharper focus if we concentrate attention on four broad strategic considerations that condition the outlook in most presidential elections, and are likely to be relevant in this one also. Then, because this is 1968, and not 1964 or 1952, there are two additional special strategic considerations to discuss — factors that could have considerable importance this year: first, the possibility that there may be no majority for President in the electoral college; and second, what the prospects are if the election of the President were to "go to the House of Representatives."

Four factors which have a powerful bearing on the over-all strategic outlook in most presidential elections are: (1) the rating given by the public to the administration in power; (2) the distribution of party identification in the United States — how many Democrats and how many Republicans there are; (3) the nature and content of the issue considerations that seem to be salient in the voters' minds; and (4) the factor that Angus Campbell and his associates at the Survey Research Center at The University of Michigan have called "candidate orientation" — the extent to which people like or dislike the presidential nominees.[1] The nature and content of all of these factors — and the party and candidate to whose advantage or disadvantage they work — can vary greatly from election to election. But in any presidential year, these four factors are likely to be important in shaping the broad outlines of the political topography over which a given electoral battle must be fought.

Public Attitudes toward the Johnson Administration

One important factor that any campaign strategist must weigh carefully in his strategic calculations this year is that the incumbent Democratic Administration of President Johnson was not wildly popular as the campaign got under way. In August, 1968, only 35 per cent of a national sample of Americans interviewed by the Gallup Poll said they approved of the way Johnson was handling his job as President — the lowest percentage since Dr. Gallup began taking these measurements of President Johnson's popularity in December, 1963. And of those interviewed in August, 1968, 52 per cent said they disapproved of Johnson's performance in the White House.

The election of 1968 thus stands in marked contrast to 1960. Then Richard Nixon, as Vice President, was running as the heir apparent of an incumbent administration led by President Eisenhower who enjoyed broad popularity. The position Vice President Humphrey finds himself in today is much less enviable; and not since 1952 has the presidential performance of the party trying to defend its control of the White House been rated so low.

The ratings that Johnson has had over the five years of his presidency are of considerable interest. (Table 1.) After enjoying extraordinarily widespread popular approval for his performance in office during the first weeks after the assassination of President Kennedy, Johnson continued to receive broadly favorable popularity ratings throughout 1964 and 1965 as his massive domestic legislative program moved through the Congress. During this period, those who approved of his performance consistently outnumbered those who disapproved by more than three to one. Then in 1966 his approval scores began to drop and

[1] Three of these factors — party identification, issues, and candidate orientation — are key variables used by the electoral analysts at the Survey Research Center in their general analysis of American electoral behavior. See Angus Campbell, Philip E. Converse, Warren E. Miller, and Donald E. Stokes, *The American Voter* (New York: John Wiley & Sons, Inc., 1960).

the disapproval percentages began to go up, so that the trend line from early 1966 to now is mostly down, with two noticeable but temporary rises in the President's popularity, in June, 1967, and April, 1968. Both of these brief rises in the President's performance rating coincided with an upsurge of hope for peace in Vietnam and elsewhere in the world. The first rise followed Johnson's June, 1967, meeting with Premier Kosygin of Russia. The second followed President Johnson's announcement on March 31, 1968, that he was ordering a substantial reduction of the bombing of North Vietnam and would not be a candidate for re-election, and the subsequent opening of the Vietnam peace talks in Paris. During the summer, however, as the peace talks appeared to be dragging on without much hope for success, Johnson's popularity again began to sag until it reached the current low point in August, 1968.

TABLE 1

President Johnson's Job Rating, 1963-1968: Responses to the Question: "Do you approve or disapprove of the way Johnson is handling his job as President?"

Date of Interviews		Approve Per Cent	Disapprove Per Cent	No Opinion Per Cent
Dec.,	1963	79	3	18
June,	1964	74	13	13
Dec.,	1964	69	18	13
July,	1965	69	19	12
Feb.,	1966 (early)	59	24	17
June,	1966 (late)	50	33	17
Dec.,	1966	48	37	15
June,	1967 (early)	44	40	16
June,	1967 (late)	52	35	13
Sept.,	1967	39	47	14
Dec.,	1967	46	41	13
Feb.,	1968	48	39	13
March,	1968 (late)	36	52	12
April,	1968	49	40	11
July,	1968	40	48	12
August,	1968	35	52	13

SOURCES: *Gallup Political Index*, Report No. 3, August, 1965, for data for Dec., 1963 through July, 1965; *Gallup Opinion Index*, Report No. 28, October, 1967, for data for Feb., 1966; and *Gallup Political Index*, Report No. 40, October, 1968, for data for June, 1966, through August, 1968.

During the current campaign, Vice President Humphrey likes to draw an analogy between this 1968 election and 1948. He is arguing that, like Harry Truman in 1948, he will confound the current polls and come from behind to win the election. A fair question, however, would be whether the more apt analogy is with 1948 or with 1952. In 1952 Adlai Stevenson had the same problem that Humphrey has today of campaigning for a party whose incumbent President's popularity is relatively low. (In 1952, only 32 per cent of Dr. Gallup's sample of prospective voters approved of the way Truman was handling his job as President.) In any event, the rating now given Lyndon Johnson is on balance working to Vice President Humphrey's disadvantage in the current campaign.

Party Identification

By contrast, party identification — the differing numbers of Americans who consider themselves Democrats, or Republicans, or independents — is a factor working to Humphrey's advantage. For many years now there have been more Democrats than Republicans; and in June of this year when the Gallup Poll asked the members of a national sample what their party identification was, 46 per cent said that they were Democrats, compared with 27 per cent who were Republicans, and 27 per cent who said they were independents. Translated into actual numbers of people, these percentages would indicate that of some 118 million Americans who are of voting age, about 54 million are Democrats, compared with 32 million Republicans, and another 32 million who are independents.[2] In other words, any election that can be transformed into a rally of the party faithful is likely to be a Democratic victory.

In an actual election situation, the Democrats' prospects are not as favorable as these party identification figures might suggest. Democrats are considerably less likely to be registered to vote than are Republicans (in August, 1968, Dr. Gallup found that 24 per cent of the Democrats were not registered to vote, compared with 16 per cent of the Republicans[3]). And even among potential voters who are registered, the Republicans are more likely actually to vote than are the Democrats. Thus, when you allow for this depreciation of the Dem-

[2] Data on the potential vote, the number of Americans of voting age, were obtained from the *Congressional Quarterly Weekly Report*, August 2, 1968, p. 2058.

[3] *The New York Times*, August 28, 1968, p. 31. Of those interviewed who said they were independents, 33 per cent said they were not registered to vote.

ocrats' natural advantage in terms of numbers, the "normal Democratic majority" in an election where on balance the short-term factors associated with the election favored neither party would fall in the vicinity of 53 per cent or 54 per cent of the vote.[4]

The election of 1960 provides an excellent example of how a progressive rallying of latent Democratic voters succeeded in producing a narrow Democratic victory. Kennedy was trailing Nixon in early September when the 1960 campaign began. But between early September and election day, support for Kennedy among persons who considered themselves Democrats rose from about 70 per cent to 84 per cent of the Democrats, and this occurred despite a religious issue which was hurting Kennedy quite seriously among Protestant Democrats. In the end Nixon was supported by 95 per cent of the Republican identifiers; but because Democrats outnumber Republicans, the support of 84 per cent of the Democrats for Kennedy was just enough to enable him to win.[5]

This normal Democratic advantage is a reflection of the enormously significant transformation in the basic loyalties of the American electorate that has taken place since the advent of the New Deal. Before

TABLE 2

The Distribution of Party Identification Among the American Electorate, 1940-1968

Year	Democrats Per Cent	Republicans Per Cent	Independents Per Cent
1940	42	38	20
1950	45	33	22
1960	47	30	23
1964	53	25	22
1966	48	27	25
June, 1968	46	27	27

SOURCES: *Gallup Opinion Index*, Report No. 28, October, 1967, for data for 1940 through 1966; *Congressional Quarterly Weekly Report*, No. 34, August 23, 1968, for data for June 1968.

[4] For a discussion of the concept of the normal Democratic vote, see Philip E. Converse, Angus Campbell, Warren E. Miller, and Donald E. Stokes, "Stability and Change in 1960: A Reinstating Election," in the *American Political Science Review*, Vol. 55, No. 2, June, 1961, pp. 273-275; and Angus Campbell, Philip E. Converse, Warren E. Miller, and Donald E. Stokes, *Elections and the Political Order* (New York: John Wiley & Sons, Inc., 1966), Chapter 2.

[5] *The Washington Post*, December 8, 1968, p. A4.

Franklin Roosevelt's day, if Dr. Gallup had been conducting public opinion polls, his findings almost certainly would have indicated that there were more Republicans than Democrats in the United States. By 1940, for which we do have Gallup Poll data, however, the Democrats slightly outnumbered the Republicans. And between 1940 and 1960, the Democratic advantage increased sharply. (Table 2.) In this year's election, the underlying partisan loyalties of the American electorate is the most important single factor helping the Democratic nominee.

The Issues of 1968

For many years the Gallup Poll has asked samples of the American public the following question: "What do you think is the most serious problem facing this country today?" Over the years the public's response to this question has varied widely, but this year there is fairly widespread agreement on what the nation's number one problem is — Vietnam. Some 51 per cent of those interviewed volunteered this response without any cue from the interviewer, a striking indication of how salient concern over the Vietnam war currently is. Crime, including riots and looting, is the second most frequently mentioned problem, at 21 per cent. And 20 per cent mentioned the problem of civil rights. (Table 3.)

It is, of course, one thing to be concerned over a problem. It may be

---

TABLE 3

The Most Important Problems Facing the United States in 1968: Responses to the Question, "What do you think is the most important problem facing this country today?"

Problem	Per Cent Mentioning the Problem*
Vietnam	51
Crime (includes looting, riots)	21
Civil Rights	20
High Cost of Living	7
Poverty	3
Other Problems	12
Don't Know	2

*The total of the percentages in this column exceeds 100 because some respondents mentioned more than one problem.

Source: The Gallup Poll, *The New York Times*, September 8, 1968, p. 77. Interviewing dates: August 8-11, 1968.

quite a different matter whether that concern is translated into a feeling that one political party or another is better equipped to cope with the problem. The Gallup Poll tries to probe into this problem, however, by asking a follow-up question to the one about the "most important problem": "Which political party do you think can do a better job of handling the problem you have just mentioned — the Republican party or the Democratic party?" Large numbers of those interviewed (38 per cent) see no difference between the parties on the issue, or are undecided. But among those expressing a preference between the parties, the Republicans are in the lead today, with 37 per cent saying the Republican party can best handle what they consider the nation's most serious problem, and 25 per cent preferring the Democrats. (Table 4.)

Which party is seen as being the party of peace? Which is the party of war? This issue dimension has also been a sensitive indicator of the mood of the electorate; and throughout most of the 1950's the Republicans, under Eisenhower's leadership, enjoyed the image of being the party of peace, a feeling that was reflected during this period in sizeable Republican pluralities in response to a Gallup Poll question: "Which political party do you think would be more likely to keep the United States out of World War III — the Republican party or the Democratic party?" Following Kennedy's election as President, the Democrats drew even with the Republicans in public responses to the question; and after the conclusion of the Cuban missile crisis in October, 1962, the Democrats took a clear lead over the Republicans as the party best suited to keep the United States out of war. This Democratic advantage widened still further when the Republicans nominated Barry Goldwater in 1964, when for a brief period the Democrats enjoyed an enormous four to one advantage over the Republicans on the issue of

---

TABLE 4

Party Seen in 1968 as Best Suited to Handle the Most Important Problem Facing the United States: Responses to the Question, "Which political party do you think can do a better job of handling the problem you have just mentioned — the Republican party or the Democratic party?"

Response	Per Cent Giving the Response
Republican party	37
Democratic party	25
No difference, undecided	38

SOURCE: The Gallup Poll, *The New York Times*, September 8, 1968, p. 77. Interviewing dates: August 8-11, 1968.

war or peace.[6] The public seems to have changed its mind again on this issue, however, and now, following nearly four years of active involvement in the Vietnam war under President Johnson, the Republicans are preferred over the Democrats as the party best suited to keep the United States out of World War III by a margin approaching two to one. (Table 5.)

If the Republicans have frequently been seen as the party of peace in the last 20 years, the Democrats are usually seen as the party that can keep the country prosperous. This is an historic advantage they have usually held ever since the enactment of the New Deal social welfare programs of Franklin Roosevelt. Yet at the moment even this normally Democratic advantage has withered away, to the point where it is currently a standoff between the Republicans and the Democrats: 36 per cent prefer the Republicans as the party that will do "the best job of keeping the country prosperous," and 36 per cent prefer the Democrats. (Table 6.) The present Democratic showing on the question concerning the maintenance of prosperity is close to the party's worst showing on the issue in the last 30 years.

During the remaining six weeks of the campaign, the Democratic party may improve its ratings on some of these issues, as the electorate, which is still predominantly Democratic, responds to the partisan stimuli of the campaign. Nevertheless, the Republicans currently enjoy a moderate advantage in terms of the short-term issue considerations of

---

TABLE 5

Party Seen in 1968 as Best Suited to Keep the United States Out of War: Responses to the Question, "Which political party do you think would be more likely to keep the United States out of World War III — the Republican party or the Democratic party?"

Response	Per Cent Giving the Response
Republican party	41
Democratic party	23
No difference, undecided	36

SOURCE: *The Gallup Poll*, The New York Times, September 8, 1968, p. 77. Interviewing dates: August 8-11, 1968.

---

6 For a useful summary of the data from 1950 through 1966 on the public's evaluation of which party was best suited to keep the United States out of war, see Nelson W. Polsby and Aaron B. Wildavsky, *Presidential Elections: Strategies of American Electoral Politics,* second edition (New York: Charles Scribner's Sons, 1964), pp. 164-165.

this particular campaign. But one should also note the large numbers of people who say there is no difference between the parties in their capacity to handle these issues, a finding which may reflect some skepticism on the part of the electorate as to whether either party has the answer to some of the problems that we face.

The Candidates

What of the voters' responses to the candidates? Is this a factor working to the Republicans' or to the Democrats' advantage? When the first report of the current election study by the Survey Research Center of The University of Michigan appears next year, we shall probably have some quite precise data on how Humphrey, Nixon, and Wallace are perceived and evaluated by the electorate. In 1956, for example, the public's attitude toward the major-party candidates was clearly a factor working to the Republicans' advantage. When voters were asked to describe what they liked or disliked about the candidates in that year, favorable references to President Eisenhower greatly outnumbered unfavorable references. For the Democratic nominee, Adlai Stevenson, by contrast, there were about as many unfavorable responses as there were favorable responses.[7] In the 1964 election, on the other hand, the voters' attitudes toward the candidates worked to the advantage of the

TABLE 6

Party Seen in 1968 as Best Suited to Keep the United States Prosperous: Responses to the Question, "Looking ahead for the next few years, which political party — the Republican or the Democratic — do you think will do the best job of keeping the country prosperous?"

Response	Per Cent Giving the Response
Republican party	36
Democratic party	36
No difference, undecided	28

Source: The Gallup Poll, The New York Times, September 8, 1968, p. 77. Interviewing dates: August 8-11, 1968.

7 Angus Campbell, Philip E. Converse, Warren E. Miller, and Donald E. Stokes, The American Voter, pp. 524-528. Voters' responses to the candidates were obtained by asking the following questions: "Now I'd like to ask you about the good and bad points of the two candidates for President. Is there anything in particular about Stevenson that might make you want to vote for him? Is there anything in particular about Stevenson that might make you want to vote against him?" Identical questions were asked about Eisenhower. Ibid., p. 226.

Democratic party. The public's references to President Johnson were predominantly positive; and unfavorable references to Senator Goldwater outnumbered the favorable references by close to two to one.[8]

Since comparable data for 1968 are not currently available, we shall have to make some guesses. The public's response to George Wallace is on balance, I think, likely to be negative. He has and will continue to have many ardent supporters. But like Goldwater in 1964 (although perhaps for different reasons), he is likely to arouse considerable apprehension among large segments of the electorate. As for the major parties, the most likely possibility is that in 1968 the factor of the public's attitudes toward the Republican and Democratic nominees will be close to a standoff. Either Nixon or Humphrey could derive some net advantage from this factor, but it is not likely to be large.

Richard Nixon is no Eisenhower. He does not appear to have the widespread personal popularity that will induce large numbers of Democrats or Independents to cross the line to vote for him as Eisenhower was able to do.[9] Humphrey by the same token does not have this kind of personal appeal to large numbers of Republicans, and the current unpopularity of the Johnson Administration with which he is associated will also not help his cause in many parts of the country. Both candidates may be seen as individuals who have worked in their respective party vineyards for two decades now, and both are probably perceived as rather partisan figures. On balance, then, this factor is probably a standoff, although the data which will be forthcoming in the future could prove that this assumption is wrong.

The Presidential Standings in September, 1968

How does the presidential race appear to be going, as of September, 1968? The voters' preferences, assuming a three-way race among Nixon, Humphrey, and Wallace, appear in Table 7. The data, drawn from six Gallup Polls, cover the voters' attitudes from May through September of this year. As of now, Nixon enjoys a sizeable lead. But the data in Table 7 also underscore a point that is often forgotten: Humphrey was even with or ahead of Nixon at the beginning of the summer. In the results released July 11th (for which the interviewing was conducted

8 Angus Campbell, "Interpreting the Presidential Victory," in Milton C. Cummings, Jr., ed., *The National Election of 1964* (Washington: The Brookings Institution, 1966), p. 259.

9 For evidence of the strength and importance of Eisenhower's personal popularity in 1956, see Angus Campbell, Philip E. Converse, Warren E. Miller, and Donald E. Stokes, *The American Voter*, pp. 525-528.

around July 1st), Gallup gave Humphrey the lead — 40 per cent to 35 per cent. It was in late July or early August, perhaps during the Republican National Convention on August 5-8, that the bottom seemed to drop out for Humphrey. In the new poll results released August 21 (polling dates: August 8-11), the standings were: Nixon, 45 per cent; Humphrey 29 per cent. Humphrey has remained behind since then; and the events at the Chicago Democratic Convention probably did little to aid his cause. But a key point to note is that his standing compared with Nixon's dropped precipitously *before* rather than after the Chicago Convention.[10]

Although the differences between Gallup's September 15 poll release and his August 21 figures are not statistically significant, there is at least a suggestion that Humphrey narrowed slightly the gap between himself and Nixon from August until September. But one thing seems clear, both from the Gallup figures and from other polls. George Wallace has been increasing his strength almost every month since late last winter. Today he attracts the support of about one voter in every five.

The Prospect of No Electoral College Majority

If Richard Nixon maintains the lead he currently has, he is virtually certain to win a clearcut majority in the electoral college, despite the prospects for a sizeable Wallace vote. But what if the gap between

---

TABLE 7

Voter Preferences in a Humphrey-Nixon-Wallace Presidential Race: The Gallup Poll Standings, May-September, 1968.

	May 12	June 12	June 23	July 11	Aug. 21	Sept. 15
Nixon	39	36	37	35	45	43
Humphrey	36	42	42	40	29	31
Wallace	14	14	14	16	18	19
Undecided	11	8	7	9	8	7

SOURCE: *Congressional Quarterly Weekly Report,* June 28, 1968, p. 1629; *Congressional Quarterly Weekly Report,* August 23, 1968, p. 2241; and *Congressional Quarterly Weekly Report,* September 27, 1968, p. 2553. Dates shown are dates on which poll results were released. The interviewing was usually conducted over a three to five day period eight to fourteen days before the release date.

---

[10] What Chicago probably did do to the Humphrey candidacy was to deprive him of the improvement in the candidate's public opinion poll standings that usually follows a major party's national convention.

Humphrey and Nixon narrows sharply? Will we then reach the situation which many view with alarm, where no presidential candidate has a clear majority in the electoral college? Such an impasse could occur, of course, and no one should discount the difficulties that our constitutional processes might encounter if this did happen. Yet the fact is that the odds are pretty strongly against one of the candidates failing to win a clear majority in the electoral college.

Let us examine the assumption on which this contention is based. First, although Wallace is strong, his support so far has not exceeded 15 per cent of the popular vote in the states outside the South. So my initial assumption is that Wallace is not going to carry any states outside the South.

If this assumption is granted, then suppose, for example, that George Wallace carried all eleven of the former states of the Confederacy — something many observers feel that Wallace will not be able to do. This would give Wallace 128 electoral votes, leaving 410 electoral votes outside the South to be divided between Nixon and Humphrey. If either major-party candidate carried 66 per cent of the electoral vote in these remaining non-southern states (270 electoral votes out of 410), then that major-party candidate would have a clear electoral college majority despite Wallace's exceptionally strong showing in the South.

At lower levels of Wallace electoral college strength, an even smaller percentage of the remaining electoral college vote would give one of the major-party candidates an electoral college majority. This point becomes clear if one imagines three different levels of electoral strength for Wallace that might be reached in this November's election:

If Wallace gets:	Wallace's electoral college vote would be:	A major-party presidential nominee would need the following percentage of the remaining electoral college vote for a majority: Per Cent Vote Necessary to Win
All 11 states of the former Confederacy	128	66 (270 of 410)
The Deep South: Ala., Ga., La., Miss., S. C.	47	55 (270 of 491)
Alabama and Mississippi	17	52 (270 of 521)

Some of the above electoral college statistics may look hard to reach, but the odds are that one of the major-party candidates will reach them — even the 66 per cent figure — because a small percentage lead in the popular vote is usually translated into a much larger percentage of the electoral college vote.[11] There are a number of examples of this "multiplier effect" as it affects the electoral college; thus Harry Truman in 1948, with 52.4 per cent of the two-party popular vote for President, got 57 per cent of the electoral college vote. Franklin Roosevelt in 1944, with 53.5 per cent of the popular vote, got over 82 per cent of the electoral college vote. And Lyndon Johnson in 1964, with 61 per cent of the popular vote, received about 90 per cent of the electoral college vote.

Even if Wallace carried all 128 southern electoral votes, if Nixon or Humphrey had about a four percentage point lead in the major-party vote in the remaining 39 states (52 per cent to 48 per cent), Nixon or Humphrey would probably have a clear electoral college majority. If Wallace carries only the five Deep South states, a two per cent lead for one of the major-party candidates in the popular vote in the remaining 45 states (51 per cent to 49 per cent) should give the presidential candidate who is in the lead a clear electoral college majority. If only Alabama and Mississippi go for Wallace, a one percentage point popular vote lead in the remaining 48 states would probably produce a clear electoral college majority.[12]

Today virtually all the national polls give Nixon a large lead over Humphrey (eight percentage points or more) in the popular vote. In

[11] For a more detailed discussion of the probable relationships between the popular vote and the electoral college vote in 1968, under various assumptions as to the Wallace strength, see the *Congressional Quarterly Weekly Report*, July 19, 1968, pp. 1816-1817.

[12] These estimates rest on the work of Professor Charles Bischoff, who has prepared a careful computer analysis of the relationship between the popular vote and the electoral college vote in the last twelve presidential elections. For a summary of Bischoff's analysis, see Neal R. Peirce, *The People's President* (New York: Simon and Schuster, 1968), pp. 141-145, and *Congressional Quarterly Weekly Report*, July 19, 1968, pp. 1816-1817. It should be noted that although the working of the electoral college system is likely to produce a clearcut winner, that electoral college winner need *not* be the candidate with the most popular votes. Bischoff estimates that in a presidential election with a plurality of about 500,000 (or 0.67 per cent based on a 75 million turnout), the popular vote winner would lose in the electoral college about one time out of three. Bischoff concluded that in an election as close as the Kennedy-Nixon contest in 1960 (plurality 112,827), there is no better than a 50-50 chance that the national electoral vote will agree with the national popular vote. *Congressional Quarterly Weekly Report, op. cit.*, p. 1817.

these circumstances, there seems to be little chance of Nixon's failing to get an electoral college majority — no matter how many states George Wallace carries in the South. If, however, the poll results in early November indicate that the popular vote gap between the two major-party presidential nominees has narrowed — particularly if the gap is four per cent or smaller — then the possibility that there may be no electoral college majority cannot be ruled out, although the odds are against it.

The Prospects If There Is No Electoral College Majority

What, then, would be the likely outcome if the election were thrown into the House? As pointed out above, this would happen only if the presidential race were close. And a close presidential race would mean that there would be no strong "presidential coattails" — a presidential sweep which incidentally sweeps many new Congressmen into office at the same time. The new Ninety-first Congress, therefore, would probably be quite similar to the present Ninetieth Congress that was elected in 1966; and since, in the election of the President in the House, every state congressional delegation has just one vote, it becomes worthwhile to determine which political party controls each of the 50 state congressional delegations.

For the present, Ninetieth Congress (which is our best guide to what the new Ninety-first Congress would be in these circumstances), the pattern of party control is as follows:

Democratic States (outside Deep South) 24
Democratic States (Deep South) 5
Republican States 18
Evenly Split State Delegations 3

As these figures indicate, Humphrey would probably have the advantage if the election were thrown into the House. At present, the Republicans control only 18 of the 50 state delegations — and the votes of 26 state delegations would be required to elect the President in the House. Even if the party control were to change (as well might happen), the Republicans have a long way to go to increase the number of delegations they control from 18 to 26. On the other hand, if the Deep South nominally Democratic state delegations were to decide to throw their support to Nixon, then Nixon might have a chance in the House. What one can be sure of is that the pressures and the bargaining would be intense if the election were thrown into the House.

My own feeling is, however, that the election will *not* be decided in the House of Representatives, even if no presidential candidate gets a clear electoral college majority. It is more likely that if there is no electoral college majority, George Wallace would, after trying to obtain whatever understandings it was possible for him to obtain, throw enough of his electoral college support to one of the major-party presidential nominees to elect Nixon or Humphrey via the electoral college route. He could, for example, hold a meeting of his electors in Montgomery, Alabama, shortly before Thanksgiving, and there, in full view of the television cameras, announce that, in order to avert a serious constitutional crisis, he has instructed his electors to cast their votes for Nixon, or for Humphrey.

There are several reasons why one might expect Wallace to behave in this fashion. First, as Richard M. Scammon has pointed out, Wallace has a more direct personal control over the probable behavior of his handpicked slates of presidential electors than he does over the Congressmen — even those from southern states — who sit in the House. The presidential electors are *his* people in a way that the Congressmen, with their own political base and their own constituencies, are not. Wallace can be surer that the presidential electors will do what he wants them to do than he can that the Congressmen will do as he wishes. Second, by behaving in this fashion, Wallace could help avert a serious constitutional crisis, and could, perhaps, get the credit for this from the American public. He could also thus be seen a decisive factor in the electoral outcome — all of which would leave him with a strong base for a future try for the Presidency in 1972. By doing this, he would appear as a responsible leader who gave the voters the opportunity to register their preferences, and then decided the final winner within the normal framework of the Constitution.[13]

Finally, there is still another reason why it looks as though Wallace would not stand by and watch the final presidential choice be transferred to the House of Representatives. Wallace, himself, has already tipped his hand as to what *he* thinks would happen if no one gets a majority in the electoral college. Wallace apparently first did this on the CBS-TV program "Face the Nation" on July 21, 1968, where he said he felt that any presidential contest in which there was an electoral college deadlock would nonetheless be decided before the election were thrown into the House.[14] But on September 8, 1968, in an inter-

[13] Richard M. Scammon, "Wallace Will Keep on Trying," *The Washington Post*, September 22, 1968, pp. B1 and B5.

[14] Wallace said on CBS-TV, "I might remind you that the electoral college meets first (before the House), and therein would lie, probably, the solution to . . . the election of the President." *Congressional Quarterly Weekly Report*, July 26, 1968, p. 1999.

view with editors and writers of *The Miami Herald,* he made the trend of his thinking even clearer. Then he declared, "I don't believe it is going to go to the House of Representatives," adding: "Well, the electoral college meets first. . . . I'd say the electoral college would settle the Presidency before it gets to the House."[15]

When asked if he expected "some bargaining" in the electoral college, Wallace replied, "I don't think it will be a 'bargaining' proposition. It will be a matter of open . . . covenants representing the viewpoint of people. If I get as many votes — popular votes — as either of the other candidates, then that group of people are entitled to have some representation in the attitude of the new administration."[16]

Whether it is called "bargaining" or "solemn covenants" (the distinction seems an elusive one), it appears that Wallace hopes to do some hard bargaining with one of the major-party presidential nominees in return for some or all of the electoral votes of Wallace presidential electors. How Mr. Nixon or Mr. Humphrey would react in such a situation, only time will tell. If we have the chance to learn the answer, however, the United States will be involved in a major constitutional crisis — a crisis which, if it occurred, could be the critical event leading to a major overhaul of the American electoral college system.[17]

SUMMARY

At the moment, however, the candidates are much more preoccupied with their current problem of winning votes. Here, in broad strategic terms, is where they appear to stand in late September, 1968. The issues of the day and the public's appraisal of the incumbent Democratic administration seem to be working to Nixon's advantage. In terms of

[15] *Congressional Quarterly Weekly Report,* September 13, 1968, p. 2444.

[16] *Ibid.,* p. 2444.

[17] In a recent Gallup Poll, a large majority of the American public favored abolishing the electoral college and electing the President by direct popular vote. The question was phrased: "Would you approve or disapprove of an amendment to the Constitution which would do away with the Electoral College and base the election of a President on the total vote cast throughout the Nation?" The results were: approve, 66 per cent; disapprove, 19 per cent; and no opinion, 15 per cent. *The Washington Post,* September 22, 1968, p. L6. However, the congressional representatives of both some of the large states and a number of the smaller states feel that the voters of their states benefit from the existing electoral college system. When various concrete alternatives to the present electoral college system are considered, agreement on which specific modification of the current system should be adopted may be difficult to obtain.

the popular appeal of the individual candidates, it is probably close to a standoff, and in some ways the candidate who is best able to get his own supporters excited about him is not Nixon, and is not Humphrey, but is George Wallace. Party identification, by contrast, is a factor working to Humphrey's advantage; and one can expect him to make a strong attempt to rally the latent Democratic majority during the final month of the campaign. As of now, Wallace's strength is holding up and Nixon is in the lead; but the gap between Humphrey and Nixon appears to be narrowing. So we could yet become involved in a surprisingly close race after what has already been an extraordinary series of surprises in this election year of 1968.

VII

SPEAKING IN THE 1968
PRESIDENTIAL CAMPAIGN

by

HAROLD F. HARDING

September, 1968

THIS PAPER *comments on the campaign concerning importance of polls, the imponderable of the Wallace campaign, the impossibility of Humphrey's position, youthful dissidence over McCarthy's come-up-pance, the credibility gap, and the uproarious events of the year 1968 to that time. Most of the paper is devoted to an evaluation of the five candidates then before the people — Wallace, Agnew, Muskie, Humphrey, and Nixon, against a backdrop of Lyndon B. Johnson — as judged by Cato's measure of an orator, "a good man speaking well." The ratings originally assigned might have been revised later, but Professor Harding has elected scrupulously to let the evaluations stand as of the day the paper was read.*

● "THERE'S NEVER BEEN a President happier in the Presidency," Hubert Humphrey said to me in the Spring of 1965, when Lyndon Johnson was still riding high. "The reason is that the President knows what to do and how to do it."

It is very unlikely that Hubert Humphrey — or anyone else would say the same thing today. For Lyndon Johnson more and more resembles the Ancient Mariner:

> God save thee, Ancient Mariner!
> From the fiends that plague thee thus! —
> Why look'st thou so? "With my crossbow,
> I shot the Albatross!"

The above quotation comes from Stewart Alsop's revealing book about "People and Power in Washington" called *The Center.*[1] The quotation is especially apt because the Albatross is the war in Vietnam — and it is the same bird and the whole record of the Johnson administration in the past four years that now plague Hubert Humphrey.

[1] Stewart Alsop, *The Center, People and Power in Washington* (New York, 1968), p. 58.

I want here to discuss him and Richard Nixon and George C. Wallace as presidential candidates. Difficult though it is to do, I want to touch upon the feature of their speaking as presidential candidates. Most of us judge candidates by television appearances. Very few persons read even snatches of speeches. Last spring I raised the question of whether campaign speaking did good or harm. Now after the spectacles at Miami and Chicago I have other questions to raise about the candidates, the way they treat the issue, the way the campaigns are run, the voter's inability to judge candidates, and the whole matter of the function of the long campaign — from primaries to the November postmortems — in the electoral process.

For all practical purposes we are told that if the election were held today Richard Nixon would win with 44 per cent of the popular vote, Wallace would get 20 per cent or more of the votes, and Humphrey about 29 per cent, and — as of now there are only 5 or 7 per cent un-decided voters. I am not one to put great faith in polls but I cannot ignore the recent trend of Humphrey down and the others up. Why is it? What became of that huge LBJ majority of 1964? How has Nixon lost some of his "loser" image? How do you account for Wallace's daily increasing popularity? Has television done all this? Are people really craving a big change in 1968? Has the Democratic party lost its "touch" as well as its grip? What makes everything so topsy-turvy?

To attempt to answer some of these questions I cannot be scientific. I certainly am not going to be a prophet. As Will Rogers used to say, "All I know is what I read in the papers" — and what people tell me. Some of these people are my students here in seminars of the past two years. I want to thank them and my colleagues in Political Science on whom I have tried out ideas.

Let me begin by making some general observations on the 1968 Campaign as of today.

1. First, the parties do not nominate the best man — whatever that may mean. The party leaders select the man they think can be elected — who will win. This prime fact is often forgotten. And I may add the matter of *who can be elected* causes wide party splits.

2. Next, the polls play a huge part in how voters make up their minds. Weak-minded voters want to be with the winners. The most recent Gallup poll, giving Nixon 43 per cent, Humphrey 31 per cent, Wallace 19 per cent, and 7 per cent undecided, has an effect that cripples the educational value of speaking about issues.

3. Again, the independents, or those who have not made up their minds, are only about half of those listed in previous years. And since the spread between Humphrey and Nixon is so great, even if Humphrey captured all the undecideds as of now he could not win.

4. George Wallace is the Big Imponderable of 1968. He has already cut painfully deeply into both parties. When Spiro Agnew recently belittled Wallace and predicted that he would only get 15 per cent of the popular vote in November, it was Agnew who was whistling Dixie.

5. The position of LBJ on the Vietnam War puts Humphrey in an impossible situation. Unless he resigns from the Vice-Presidency and repudiates the Johnson administration he must go through the motions of defending his leader, the man who made him Vice-President. Hubert is walking on a tight rope across the Grand Canyon.

6. The Young People who followed McCarthy from the snows of New Hampshire to the Chicago Convention have created a vigorous new element in American politics that cannot be reached by old-fashioned ways. McCarthy's vacation on the French Riviera is not helping the Democratic cause. It is a paradox that Humphrey, the darling of the liberals in 1948, one of the founders of the Americans for Democratic Action, and a man with superb liberal record, is now unable to cash in on his past — because he is Vice-President of the LBJ Corporation — formerly called Consensus Unlimited. It will be a major miracle if Humphrey and Muskie can win over a high proportion of first-time voters this year.

7. Johnson created the Credibility Gap. Now we have an Audibility Gap and Comprehensibility Gap. In this campaign many, many voters have already made up their minds. They do not listen to the candidates. And except in the case of George Wallace voters do not understand what the big party leaders are talking about. What is worse they do not want to understand. Senator Muskie summed it all up when he recently said, "I've never seen a year or a campaign when ideas get so tangled up with words." This year a vast number of Americans do not believe, they do not listen, they do not understand — and they are deeply frustrated.

8. What has caused all this confusion, this lack of trust, this shortage of faith in the two-party system, this disarray we find ourselves in? It would be easy to blame it on television, or the Negroes, or Rising Taxes, or Rising Expectations, or Unfulfilled Promises, or a breakdown of Law and Order. All these do enter into it. The Vietnam War has profoundly affected our emotions. I like to think that we lack good explainers in both parties. The result is a heightening of suspicion — the like of which I have never seen before in my lifetime.

These eight points do not cover the whole background of our political woes as we must face them in the next six weeks. There are many problems that I cannot discuss for lack of time. Let me just say that I fear it will be more and more difficult for rational speech-making to get through to the average or sub-average American voter. The feelings are too high for, to use Adlai Stevenson's 1952 phrase, "talking sense to the American People."

Nevertheless this will be my main purpose here. I cannot tell you that speaking is unimportant — though I have some evidence to support that view. What I really want to do is to characterize for you the speakers and their speeches as of today. I will talk about five candidates — because, as far as I know, the American Independent party still has only a "stand-in" candidate for the Vice-Presidency. I will discuss the five[2] in this order: Wallace, Agnew, Muskie, Humphrey, and Nixon.

Here are some generalizations about the group as a whole: four are lawyers by training. Humphrey studied pharmacy and took a master's degree at Lousiana State University in political science. Wallace and Agnew did not complete four years of college — but do have law degrees. Three of the five are ex-college debaters — Nixon at Whittier, Humphrey at Minnesota, and Muskie at Bates College, Maine. Four are veterans of World War II. Only Humphrey did not serve in World War II. He was reminded of this during the West Virginia primary in 1960. All five are what we could call professional politicians. They have been in public office most of their lives. In the case of Wallace he got around the two-term limit for Governor of Alabama by having his wife, Lurleen, run for Governor.

Of the five — Agnew, Humphrey, Wallace, and Muskie have had experience at both the legislative and the executive levels. Except for the Vice-Presidency Nixon has always served as a legislator. I cannot refrain from recalling what President Eisenhower once said when asked what important decisions Nixon had helped him make, "If you'll give me a week I may be able to recall some."

Humphrey and Muskie are members of Phi Beta Kappa and of Delta Sigma Rho, the honorary debate fraternity. Nixon is now a New York lawyer — making probably $250,000 a year and is the only near million-aire of the group. He has come a long way from that day in 1952 when he asked for pity because of his wife's cloth coat and the dog, Checkers, that was given to him and that he was not going to give back.

[2] At the time this paper was delivered, General Curtis LeMay had not been chosen as Wallace's running mate.

The records of Nixon and Humphrey in the Senate and as the Senate's presiding officer are easy to examine and they are crystal clear. Humphrey cast his vote as a *liberal* to break four historic ties. Nixon as Vice-President voted eight times to break tie votes, and ten times as a Senator he did not vote on tie votes. On nine occasions as a Senator Humphrey did not vote on tie votes. What do we make of this? Well, you have to look into the bills proposed to decide. I will give you some examples: In February, 1960, Nixon voted to block reconsideration of a proposal to authorize increased aid for school construction and teachers' salaries. In May of this year Humphrey cast the forty-third "yea" vote to break a 42-42 tie vote holding up an urgent Supplemental Appropriation Bill to appropriate $25 million for the Office of Economic Opportunity's Head Start program. It is unfair to stop with only these two examples. I think it is not unfair to say that Humphrey has consistently been for liberal causes and he has been a prime mover, an initiator, and an expediter of liberal legislation. His record has been pro-civil rights and pro-labor all the way. After his defeat for the governorship of California, Mr. Nixon has been accepting retainers from America's big corporations.

What about these five men as orators? I define the orator as a "good man speaking well" — *Vir bonus dicendi peritus,* as Marcus Cato said. He may not always be on the winning side. But he uses logical, emotional, and ethical appeals in good proportions as available means of persuasion. Of the three his *ethos,* his integrity, his personal character and reputation are by far more significant than the man's voice or his clever use of words.

I have to go back to the Fifth Century B. C., for one of my ideal orators. I mean Pericles. In words that I greatly esteem, Thucydides in the *History of the Peloponnesian War* describes the ideal statesman, supposedly in the words of Pericles. The occasion was 430 B.C., and Pericles was speaking in the Athenian Ecclesia to a war-weary people. Here is what he said:

> And yet if you are angry with me, it is with one who, as I believe, is second to no man either in knowledge of the proper policy, or in the ability to expound it, and who is moreover not only a patriot but an honest one. A man possessing that knowledge without that faculty of exposition might as well have no idea at all on the matter: if he had both these gifts, but no love for his country, he would be but a cold advocate for her interests; while were his patriotism not proof against bribery, everything would go for a price.[3]

3 *The Complete Writings of Thucydides,* Edited by John H. Finley, Jr., Modern Library (New York, 1954), Book II, Ch. 60, p. 116.

There is the blueprint for the ideal orator-statesman: one who knows the proper policy, has an ability to explain it, is a patriot, and an honest man.

I want to use these qualifications to measure the various candidates. Please remember that I give my personal opinions only. In some cases my evidence is scanty and I have to rely on hunches. I am an old man and although I have been fooled many times in my life I hope a politician has to work harder now to "take me in" than the politicians of forty years ago.

GEORGE C. WALLACE

To me George Wallace is a man of narrow and limited vision on policies at the national and international levels. His speech is ideal for poorly educated persons. He may or may not have had good policies as Governor of Alabama. Even if he was a big fish in that job I know he would be devoured in the Presidential Ocean.

As a speaker he is clever, quick-witted, sharp-tongued and enormously cocky. He handles hecklers with ease — of course he stands behind a bullet-proof lectern. The man talks fast, uses folksy appeals, and slips in and out of spurious ideas with a straight face. The people who listen to George Wallace love his style. He does what many very ordinary men wish they could do — argue against the ontide of Civil Rights legislation by the Federal Government. I heard Wallace speak to a hostile audience a few years ago — long before his present popularity. In the end students grudgingly gave him their quiet attention. This is something even Hubert Humphrey has had trouble doing of late. When George Wallace spoke to the American Legion in New Orleans recently he was repeatedly interrupted by applause and laughter (thirty-five times). The columnists, Robert S. Allen and John A. Goldsmith, report:

> Between his pointed sallies, however, Wallace became an urbane, soft-spoken lecturer who might have been a bureaucrat himself. Some delegates found that transition confusing and a few wondered whether Wallace had toned down his much publicized remarks a bit for his Legion audience.[4]

When Wallace was interviewed by David Frost on the Westinghouse Presidential Debate 1968 program he was truculent, evasive, and at times incomprehensible in his answers. He repeatedly denied he was a racist and refused to discuss the Negro problem at all.

Recalling Pericles's specifications of the ideal statesman, I would have to say that George Wallace does not know high-level policy, and

4 *El Paso Times,* 18 September 1968.

he cannot cogently explain to educated persons what he does proclaim; he may be a patriot in a narrow sort of way, but I have some doubts about his being an honest one. He used a force of Alabama statetroopers on his early campaign, and he put the bite hard on Alabama businessmen for his campaign funds. I would rate Wallace about 20 per cent on a scale of 100. But his ability to gain votes among the less discriminating grows every day.

SPIRO T. AGNEW

You have all heard that Agnew admitted at the Miami Convention that his name was not exactly a household word. He was the surprise unknown of the possible candidates. He was chosen, some say, by or with the approval of Strom Thurmond, as the man least offensive to the left and right wings of the Republican party. On the surface his record makes Agnew appear to be a liberal. He is described as an expert on urban affairs, civil rights and minority groups, and law and order. He has accused Hubert Humphrey as being "squishy soft" on Communism — but then retracted. It appears now that Agnew's role is that of hatchet man for Nixon — who is trying to be mild and unprovocative in his own speaking.

Not having heard Agnew make a full length speech as yet I cannot really judge the man. But I did listen to his hour-long television interview. As you know a man's eyes give many signals — some good and some bad. Whenever Agnew answers a question or concludes his point he closes his eyes, tilts his head with an air of finality approaching the pontifical. I found it at first amusing, then annoying, and soon a bit disgusting. But I am very finicky about mannerisms of speakers.

For me Agnew is a small-calibre politician thrust into a role far beyond his qualifications. By the Periclean standard, he does not know much policy, he speaks in platitudes, he is a parochial sort of patriot, and I judge him to be honest. He sold some property near a new Chesapeake Bay bridge-site — at a loss — to avoid the charge of profiting. I rate Agnew at about the 40 per cent level.

EDMUND S. MUSKIE

Up until a month ago Senator Muskie was hardly any better known than Spiro Agnew. Professional Senate watchers know him, however, and Stewart Alsop rated him among the 22 Very Able United States Senators. I might add that Alsop lists 45 Able Senators and does not even mention the 33 remaining. Alsop explains what he means by the "Club" in the Congress — which he calls "the official hierarchy of both parties in both houses; the chairmen of the important standing committees plus most of the ranking minority members of the standing committees." Alsop wrote as of last spring:

> There are also one or two, notably in the Senate — like Senator Edmund Muskie of Maine or Senator John Stennis of Mississippi or Senator John Pastore of Rhode Island — who have no exalted standing in the hierarchy or key committee chairmanships, but who are members of the Congressional ruling class for reasons of personality, intelligence, energy, or absorption in the affairs of Congress.[5]

Muskie's reputation did not come overnight. He was attractive to Humphrey on the basis of well-earned merit. And Lyndon Johnson unwittingly put him there. Back in 1952 the freshman senators were asked to express their committee preferences. They each named six committees and expected to get on three. Then LBJ, the Majority Leader, sent around word requesting new senators to tell how they planned to vote on a change in the Senate rules to limit filibuster. The freshman Senator Muskie reportedly replied, "You'll know when I cast my vote," and then sided with Senate liberals against Johnson to limit debate. Muskie found that when the committee assignments were handed out, he had been refused his first three choices of committees and instead was given his fourth, fifth, and sixth choices: The Banking and Currency, Public Works, and Government Operations Committees. I should add that freshmen Senators Dodd, Byrd, and McGee were all awarded seats on the powerful Appropriations Committee. They had voted for LBJ against liberalizing the rules.

Edmund Muskie, whom I have heard only in television interviews and in portions of speeches, does have a surprising command of policy matters. He explains exceedingly well. In fact, he has made his mark as the man who does his homework.

The best early portrait is to be found in the illuminating article by Martin Nolan, "Muskie of Maine," published in *The Reporter* for July 13, 1967. I have time only to review it briefly. It tells how Muskie won his spurs by thorough study of the facts, by persistence, and by courtesy towards his opposition. His "star legislative performance" came in August, 1966, when Senator Ribicoff was examining "The Federal role in urban affairs."

President Johnson was trying to gain support for the Model Cities bill, the first major proposal of the Department of Housing and Urban

5 Alsop, *op. cit.*, p. 296.

Development. At the start Senator Muskie was critical of HUD's presentation. It was both too vague and too technical. He suggested two new sections to allow smaller cities to obtain money for urban planning and to encourage "the preservation of historic buildings in towns and cities."

For two days Muskie spoke to the Senate on matters of quiet complexity while the Ribicoff hearings thrashed about in kleig-lit confusion. But the senators were listening to Muskie. He spent most of his time detailing who would get what in the bill, but also spoke of philosophical considerations: "The pages of history are full of the tales of those who sought the promise of the city and found only despair. From the Book of Job to Charles Dickens, to James Baldwin, we have read the ills of the cities. Our cities contain within themselves the flower of man's genius and the nettles of his failures." This won the approval of Albert Gore (D. Tennessee), who said that Muskie spoke "with a clarity, elocution, articulateness, and grammatical perfection that few Senators possess." Muskie replied: "I thank the Senator from Tennessee. I was really trying to sell the program and not the speaker."[6]

When the Model Cities bill passed the Senate by a vote of 52-22 the Majority Leader, Senator Mike Mansfield, gave Muskie the highest praise. Senator Clark of Pennsylvania said what was so remarkable was that Senator Muskie "does not come from an urban area." Republican senators admitted that Senator Muskie had won them over. Senator Robert F. Kennedy (D., New York) called Muskie's effort "the best speech I ever heard in the Senate." Weeks later a cabinet officer confided: "If you have a domestic bill that's really tough and you need advice on how to get it through, Ed Muskie's the best guy up there."

Is it any wonder that Hubert Humphrey selected Edmund Muskie as his running mate?

Muskie has helped push through President Johnson's anti-pollution program, the Water Quality Act of 1965, and the Clean Air Act of 1965. I like to think that some of Muskie's skill comes from his training as a debater at Bates College in Maine, long famous for its superior debate teams, and from his moot court experience at Cornell Law School. He easily rates high marks as a patriot and an honest one. Any Democrat who can snag Republican votes in the State of Maine must have some special qualifications. I regard Edmund Muskie as the best qualified man intellectually and in other ways for the Presidency. I know full well that being intellectual is not the *sine qua non* for the presidency. Nevertheless, I give him the only *cum laude* in the group.

6 *The Reporter*, July 13, 1967, pp. 45-46.

HUBERT H. HUMPHREY

To go now to the Democratic nominee for the Presidency is a big leap. In theory he should be the best qualified speaker of the lot. He has been and is now within a heart-beat of the Presidency. He has a sixteen-year record as a liberal legislator, and before that he was the best mayor Minneapolis ever had. He is a practical, working politician with both virtues and some faults. He probably talks too much — is glib and effusive when the occasion may call for brevity and restraint. He is too willing perhaps to discuss any problem — you name it. This year he was rejected by the Americans for Democratic Action in favor of Senator McCarthy. But recently the Americans for Democratic Action repented and reversed itself. His phrase, "the politics of joy," has backfired. His name-calling, frantic question-answer style of campaigning has cast doubts among his friends. He has been cold-shouldered by President Johnson, and his Vietnam troop deployment ideas have been counter-stated by LBJ. His urgent plea to debate Nixon on television has been rebuffed. Nixon's friends in Congress have thwarted the legislation needed to suspend section 315 of the law requiring networks to give equal time to all candidates.

In my opinion the American voter honestly needs the opportunity to see Nixon, Humphrey, and Wallace all together on the same program or on several programs. They should be limited in discussion to such topics as the war in Vietnam, our new needs for a policy of National Security, and a domestic problem like Crime in the Streets, Inflation and Surtaxes, or Civil Rights. The present campaign has produced little real conception among us of the candidates' stands on these matters in the past four weeks. Do you know where Nixon and Humphrey stand on the issues of most concern to you?

I should warn that in such a confrontation George Wallace might come off better with the lower mass of voters than either Humphrey or Nixon. Mr. Nixon's present strategy of dragging his feet about debates is in direct contrast to his earlier willingness to meet the opposition. I had a letter from a Nixon aide last April saying that Mr. Nixon would be glad to debate any Democrat, but he refused to debate fellow Republicans.

We, the voters, must demand a far higher plane of discussion in the campaign than the candidates have so far provided. They are acting like neophyte high school debaters. To date I have not heard a single speech that can compare with any of Adlai Stevenson's 1952 speeches. The educational process which the campaign should provide has been a mockery. It may be too much to expect a campaigner to act like a statesman but he should occasionally reveal that he has the capacity for becoming one. How else can we judge a man unless we heed the high standards of Pericles — a knowledge of the policy required and a strong ability to explain it? George Wallace's efforts to answer Martin Agronsky last Sunday afternoon constitute an insult to the intelligence of the American voter.

But to get back to Hubert Humphrey. He does have the ability to speak well on the superior knowledge he has — his position has given him the best opportunity to learn our capabilities and our intentions. Why has he flubbed so badly? Why does LBJ seem to be hindering the party rather than helping it? Why has Congress failed to make quorum calls of late? Why have our able negotiators in Paris been so hobbled? Why did LBJ call Mr. Nixon and Mr. Agnew for briefings to the Ranch two days after their nominations?

The lack of good answers to these questions may suggest why Vice-President Humphrey has been so ineffective to date. Should we believe him or the President of the United States?

The answer lies in a broader perspective. We have been expecting the impossible of Hubert Humphrey — to repudiate his leader. It was LBJ, you remember, who personally nominated Humphrey in Atlantic City in 1964 in these words as recorded in the *New York Times:*

> Every step of Humphrey has been marked by excellence and achievement. . . . I will feel strengthened knowing that he is at my side at all times in the great work of your country and your government. . . . This is not a sectional choice, a way to balance the ticket. This is simply the best man in America for this job.

Humphrey was nominated by acclamation in 1964. I believe he deserved it. His Senate record as an energetic, progressive legislator can hardly be equaled either in quality or quantity.

Humphrey has been accused by his liberal friends in the Americans for Democratic Action of going conservative and becoming Johnson's man. In a moment I will explain how the voter who is now disenchanted with the man must become open-minded. The campaign still has six weeks to go. We should not try to cast ballots for anyone today. There are too many imponderables before us that can change opinions right up to the moment we enter the voting booths.

RICHARD M. NIXON

Nixon's acceptance speech at Miami has been acclaimed as one of his best. It was indeed well received and did present a new Nixon — and probably not the last version of newness. A few days ago Nixon spoke on the office of the Presidency and some writers are calling this speech his best. Having read only excerpts of the speech and one reporter's account I cannot really judge the work. But let me read a few Nixon sentences:

> The President has a duty to decide, but the people have a right to know why. The President has a responsibility to tell them, to lay out all the facts and explain not only why he chose as he did but also what it means to the future. Only through an open, candid dialogue with the people can a President maintain this trust and leadership.[7]

My quarrel with Richard Nixon — and Hubert Humphrey, too — is that they have not followed this prescription in the campaign so far. One is as bad as the other. Both can do far better as explainers than they are doing as evaders. Both are former debaters and they know about issues, proofs, and rebuttals. So far they have been making charges, counter-charges, and calling each other names. I resent their puerile conduct.

Let me go back to Nixon at Miami. *The Saturday Review*[8] has printed excerpts from Nixon's acceptance that bear remarkable resemblances to paragraphs from John F. Kennedy and Martin Luther King. The language is not identical but close enough to warrant the use of the word *plagiarism*. When the president of an Ivy League university was accused of stealing the words and ideas of another college president for his Inaugural Address some years ago, he blamed his ghost writer. But Mr. Nixon boasted that he wrote his own speech — as he usually does.

This incident harks back to the Tricky Dick image Nixon has been trying for years to shake. Can you believe what he says? Is he really concerned about Negroes, civil rights, a minimum wage for labor, the poverty program, and the unrest among college students and faculties? Could he get through the kind of legislation that LBJ put through — if he wanted to do it? Would the country really be better off if we went back to the Eisenhower years — the golden age of Republicanism?

Nixon's acceptance speech has now been condensed in the October 1968 Reader's Digest under the title, "Let a New Day Dawn for the U.S.A." It is actually better than the original — but even so I find the style artificial, the sentiment corny, and the substance like puffed rice.

[7] Richard Nixon, "The Nature of the Presidency," in *Vital Speeches*, October 15, 1968, pp. 6-8, at p. 6.

[8] "The Rhetoric of the New Nixon," *The Saturday Review*, August 24, 1968, p. 22.

But all this is because I did not admire Nixon in 1960 and I do not admire him now. You may chalk this up to prejudice — faculty prejudice if you like. I belong to the same kind of group that at Duke University, his law school alma mater, voted against awarding Richard Nixon an honorary degree several years ago.

But I am sorely disappointed in both men in this campaign. They may have served well as Vice-Presidents but *up to now* I find myself unable to vote for either man. Three years ago I would have unhesitatingly voted for Humphrey. I hope that the intellectual level of the campaign speaking before November 5 will help me make a clear-conscience choice.

LYNDON B. JOHNSON

This is the year when millions of Americans are voting AGAINST something — a man, a set of issues, a record, or promises unkept. Although he renounced his candidacy on March 31, LBJ is very much in the campaign. He is the shadow behind all Democrats this year. The disillusioned Democrats, the Conservative Republicans, the inflamed friends of George Wallace, are all voting *against* LBJ. Humphrey inherits the brunt of this opposition. I doubt whether, even if he could make Adlai Stevenson-type speeches from now until election day, he could erase the stigma he bears. But I have not given up hope.

Meanwhile, LBJ's future role in the campaign is unknown. He has made one ten-minute radio speech. Art Buchwald suggested the other day that the television debates should be between Johnson and Humphrey. This might be helpful.

Johnson is a proud and sensitive man, a man who craves to be liked but is disliked even by his close associates. Let me read the March 1968 words of Warren Weaver, Jr., of the *New York Times:*

> Brusque, demanding, arbitrary, alternately secretive and effusive, Johnson has proved a difficult man for the voters to love, but his experience, political cunning, and unflinching leadership towards the goals as he sees them may prove sufficient to overcome a non-charismatic personality.[9]

That was surely written before March 31. I doubt whether more of Johnson's speaking can help Humphrey now. And perhaps this is the real reason why Humphrey may not have urged him.

If the Democrats lose in 1968 it will be explained in the same way that Goldwater lost in 1964. Millions will express their protest by voting for Nixon or Wallace or by not voting at all.

9 *New York Times Election Handbook,* 1968, p. 24.

Johnson was a superb parliamentarian in the Senate but he has been a failure in the second half of his Presidential term. He has not been a good explainer in the Periclean sense and the doubt about the lack of wisdom of his policies grows every day. Stewart Alsop tells how Johnson recalls his high school debating days in these words:

> "We won sixty-five of sixty-six debates, only lost the last one. We won the city and the county championship, but we lost the state, by a vote of the judges of three to two. We were on the wrong side. We had the affirmative of 'Resolved, that the "jury system be abolished."' I was so disappointed that I went right into the bathroom and was sick."
>
> There was not a flicker of a smile on his face as he recalled the long-ago moment when, in the horror and pain of failure, he vomited in the bathroom.[10]

It may well be that historians of ten years from now will have to recount that once again LBJ won most of his struggles as President — except the last one. As a speaker Johnson has not always been "the good man speaking well." To use the current vogue-word, there has been a certain "erosion" in his posture as judged by the Periclean standards.

One of our speakers in this Symposium, Milton Cummings, edited the final book of that distinguished Harvard political scientist, V. O. Key, Jr., called *The Responsible Electorate: Rationality in Presidential Voting 1936-1960.* A main thesis of the book is that the American voter is not a pawn manipulated by campaign strategists and party chiefs. Key does not underestimate the good sense of the mass of voters. Only time will tell what is good sense in the 1968 election. The decision will rest on the returns late on the night of November 5. The real appraisal must await the administration of the man elected. Four years ago LBJ won 61 per cent of the popular vote. Now he is at the lowest ebb of his popularity. The question becomes: will the rejection of LBJ as inherited by Hubert Humphrey be evidence of the responsibility of the electorate — or of their *irresponsibility?*

[10] Alsop, *op. cit.,* p. 60.

CONTRIBUTORS

MILTON C. CUMMINGS, JR., was born in New Haven, Connecticut, in 1933. He is now Professor of Political Science at Johns Hopkins University. His bachelor of arts degree is from Swarthmore; he was a Rhodes Scholar and was awarded the bachelor of philosophy degree from Oxford University; his doctor's degree was earned at Harvard University. His publications are *Congressmen and the Electorate*, 1966; *The National Election of 1964* (Editor), 1966; *The Image of the Federal Service* (Co-author), 1964; and *Source Book of a Study of Occupational Values and the Image of the Federal Service* (Co-author), 1964.

HAROLD F. HARDING was born in Niagara Falls, New York, in 1903. He is H. Y. Benedict Professor of Speech and Rhetoric at The University of Texas at El Paso. His bachelor's degree was earned at Hamilton College and his master's and doctor's degrees at Cornell University. He served ten years at George Washington University and twenty years at Ohio State University as Professor of Speech. He served in the United States Army Reserve from 1927 to 1964, and rose from the rank of private to that of Major General. Some of his publications are *Lectures on Rhetoric and Belles Lettres* by Hugh Blair, with a Critical Introduction by H. F. Harding (2 vols.), 1965; *A Source Book of Creative Thinking* (Co-author), 1962; and *The Age of Danger, Major Speeches on American Problems*, 1952.

STANLEY KELLEY, JR., is Professor at Princeton University. He was born in Detroit, Kansas, in 1926. He received bachelor's and master's degrees from the University of Kansas and the Ph.D. from Johns Hopkins University. He is the author of *Professional Public Relations and Political Power*, 1956; *Political Campaigning*, 1960; and co-author of *Presidential Election and Transition 1960-61*, 1961, and *The National Election of 1964*, 1966.

JASPER B. SHANNON was born in Carlisle, Kentucky, in 1903. His degrees are from Transylvania College and the University of Wisconsin. His principal professorial service has been rendered to the University of Nebraska, where he is now, and to the University of Kentucky, but he has taught also at the University of Michigan, Johns Hopkins, and Transylvania. He has been President of the Southern Political Science Association and of the Midwestern Conference of

Political Scientists. He is the author of *Money and Politics*, 1959; *Towards a New Politics in the South*, 1949; *The Study of Comparative Government* (Editor and Co-author), 1949; *Presidential Politics in Kentucky* (Co-author), 1951; and *Personal Ambition as a Factor in Politics*, 1964.

AARON WILDAVSKY is Professor of Political Science and Chairman of the Department at the University of California at Berkeley. He was born in New York City in 1930. He took his bachelor's degree from Brooklyn College and his master's and doctor's degrees from Yale University. He has taught at Oberlin College and has served in various political research capacities for the government of the United States. His published books are *The Politics of the Budgetary Process*, 1964; *Leadership in a Small Town*, 1964; *Dixon-Yates: A Study in Power Politics*, 1962; *Studies in Australian Politics: the 1926 Referendum*, 1958; and *Presidential Elections* (Co-author), 1964.

JAMES C. WRIGHT, JR., is a Democratic Member of the United States Congress from Fort Worth. He was born in the city he serves in 1922, and he was educated in the Fort Worth and Dallas public schools and at Weatherford College and the University of Texas at Austin. He served in the Texas Legislature and as Mayor of Weatherford, Texas. He was elected to Congress in 1954 and has since been re-elected biennially. He is a lay worker in the Presbyterian Church.